# SRA
## BUILDING
# Vocabulary
## *Skills*

## Level 1
## Student Edition

McGraw Hill **SRA**

Columbus, Ohio

**SRAonline.com**

Send all inquiries to:
SRA/McGraw-Hill
4400 Easton Commons
Columbus, OH 43219-6188

ISBN: 978-0-07-623552-0
MHID: 0-07-623552-1

1 2 3 4 5 6 7 8 9 QWD 16 15 14 13 12 11 10 09

The **McGraw·Hill** Companies

# Table of Contents

# Unit 3

# Unit 4

# "Let's Read" Vocabulary

**1** **Word Meanings**

## Examples

1. page      guess

2. page      finish

3. about      circle

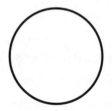

4. speak      ready

5. sentence      finish

6. circle      begin

Score _____
(Top Score 6)

**Teacher** Read each pair of words aloud. Have students cirlce the vocabulary word that matches the example picture.

| Vocabulary List | 3. page | 7. ready |
|---|---|---|
| | 4. about | 8. circle |
| 1. sentence | 5. guess | 9. speak |
| 2. begin | 6. finish | 10. story |

"Let's Read" Vocabulary • Word Meanings

## ② Reference Skills

## Alphabetical Order

1.

2.

3.

4.

5.

**Teacher** Read each word aloud. Have students trace the first letter of each word. Point out that the words are in alphabetical order.

Score _____
(Top Score 5)

## ③ Build New Vocabulary

## More Than One

1. circle**s**

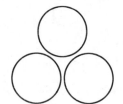

2. sentence**s**

3. picture**s**

4. page**s**

5. book**s**

6. artist**s**

Score _____
(Top Score 6)

**Teacher** Read the plural form of each word aloud. Have students trace the letter *s* at the end of each word to make the word plural.

| Vocabulary List | 3. page | 7. ready |
|---|---|---|
| 1. sentence | 4. about | 8. circle |
| 2. begin | 5. guess | 9. speak |
| | 6. finish | 10. story |

## Word Play

## Synonyms

1. begin

start

eat

2. finish

game

end

3. circle

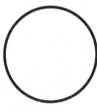

sphere

triangle

4. speak

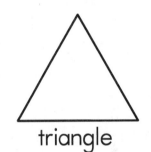

play

talk

5. story

radio

tale

**Teacher** Read each word aloud. Have students draw a circle around the word/picture combination that means the same as the vocabulary word.

Score _____
(Top Score 5)

# Vocabulary About Books
## 1 Word Meanings

## Show the Meaning

1. paper

○ ○ ○

2. ink
 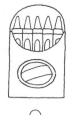 
○ ○ ○

3. bookend
  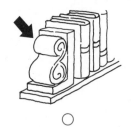
○ ○ ○

4. study

○ ○ ○

5. backpack

○ ○ ○

Score _____
(Top Score 5)

**Teacher** Read each word aloud. Have students fill in the bubble below the picture that best matches the word.

| Vocabulary List | 3. due | 7. borrow |
|---|---|---|
| 1. study | 4. backpack | 8. return |
| 2. bookend | 5. ink | 9. print |
| | 6. fine | 10. paper |

# ❷ Reference Skills

## Alphabet Match

1. borrow                     b

2. return                     d

3. due                        f

4. fine                       i

5. print                      p

6. ink                        r

**Teacher** Read each word aloud. Have students draw a line from the word to its beginning letter.

Score _____
(Top Score 6)

## 3 Build New Vocabulary

# Compound Words

1. bookstore

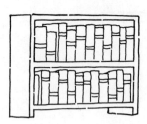

2. bookmark

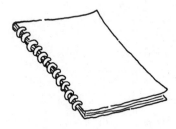

3. bookshelf

4. notebook

The
Three
Little
Pigs

5. storybook

BOOKS GALORE

Score _____
(Top Score 5)

**Teacher** Read each word aloud.
Have students draw a line from
the word to the picture that
best matches.

| Vocabulary List | 3. due | 7. borrow |
|---|---|---|
| 1. study | 4. backpack | 8. return |
| 2. bookend | 5. ink | 9. print |
| | 6. fine | 10. paper |

**Word Play**

## Words in Words

1. borrow

2. return

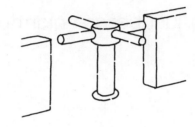

3. fine

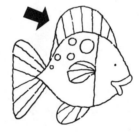

4. paper

5. print

**Teacher** Read each word aloud. Tell students to listen carefully to the hints and look at the pictures. Then have them circle each hidden word. Hints are in the *Teacher's Edition* on page 9.

Score _____
(Top Score 5)

# Vocabulary for Time

**1** Word Meanings

## Definitions

1. present
   - ○ going on now
   - ○ not ever happening

2. dawn
   - ○ just before nightfall
   - ○ the time when light appears in the morning

3. always
   - ○ at all times
   - ○ once in a while

4. past
   - ○ a time that has gone by
   - ○ at this minute

5. instant
   - ○ a very long amount of time
   - ○ a very short amount of time

6. daily
   - ○ every day
   - ○ once a week

Score _____
(Top Score 6)

**Teacher** Read each word and definition aloud. Have students fill in the bubble next to the correct definition of the word.

| Vocabulary List | 3. daily | 7. minute |
|---|---|---|
| 1. present | 4. suddenly | 8. always |
| 2. instant | 5. already | 9. past |
| | 6. sometime | 10. dawn |

## Reference Skills

## Which Comes First?

| a b c d e f g h i j k l m n o p q r s t u v w x y z |
| --- |

1. daily          always          finish

2. dawn          instant          guess

3. present          past          minute

4. suddenly          past          sentence

5. sometime          begin          already

**Teacher** Read each set of words aloud. Tell students to look at each beginning letter. Have them draw a circle around the word that would come first in the dictionary.

Score _____
(Top Score 5)

## Build New Vocabulary

## Organizing Time

1. second → _minute_ → hour

2. _____ _day_ → week →

_month_ → year

3. past → _present_ → future

4. _____ _daily_ → weekly → monthy

Score _____
(Top Score 5)

**Teacher** Have students read
each linear graph and then trace
each missing word.

| Vocabulary | 3. daily | 7. minute |
|---|---|---|
| **List** | 4. suddenly | 8. always |
| 1. present | 5. already | 9. past |
| 2. instant | 6. sometime | 10. dawn |

Vocabulary for Time • Build New Vocabulary

## Word Play

# Same or Different?

1. past       present              S       D

2. always     sometime             S       D

3. dawn       morning              S       D

4. daily      suddenly             S       D

5. already    past                 S       D

**Teacher** Read each pair of words aloud. Tell students to decide if the words have the same meaning or different meanings. Have them draw a circle around the *S* if the meanings are the same or around the *D* if the meanings are different.

Score _____
(Top Score 5)

# "Family" Vocabulary

## 1  Word Meanings

## Word Web

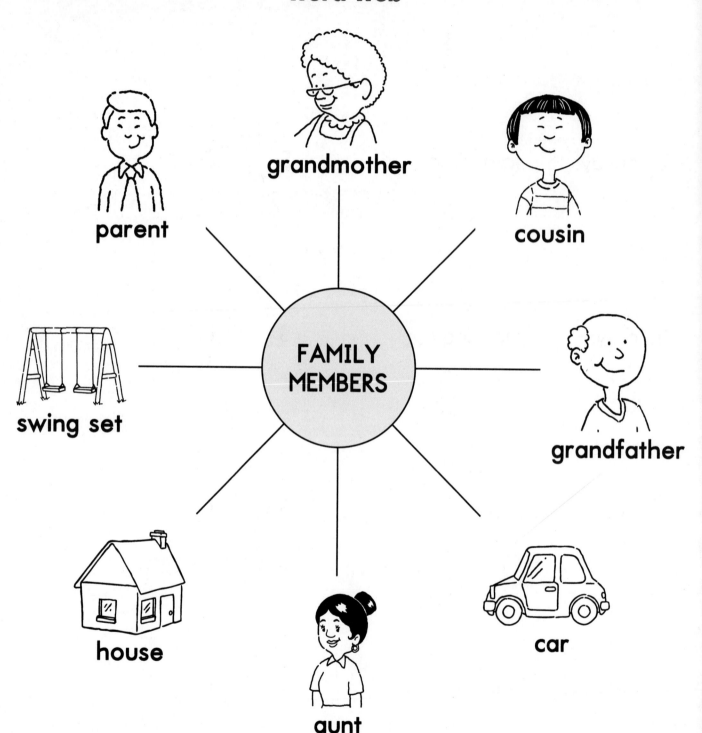

parent

grandmother

cousin

swing set

FAMILY
MEMBERS

grandfather

house

aunt

car

Score _____
(Top Score 5)

**Teacher** Tell students to look at each picture in the word web. Have them draw a circle around the pictures that represent members of a family.

| Vocabulary List | | |
|---|---|---|
| 1. belong | 3. grandfather | 7. support |
| 2. parent | 4. child | 8. cousin |
| | 5. members | 9. related |
| | 6. grandmother | 10. depend |

**②** **Reference Skills**

## Beginning Letters

1.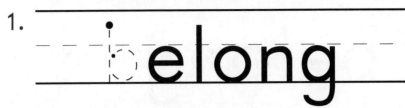

I belong to that family.

2.

My uncle's son is my cousin.

3.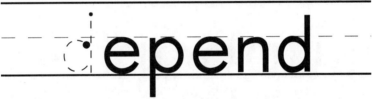

We depend on family to take care of us.

4.

There are five members in my family.

5.

To support someone is to help him or her.

**Teacher** Read each word and sentence aloud. Have students trace the beginning letter of each word. Help students notice that the words are in alphabetical order.

Score _____
(Top Score 5)

## ③ Build New Vocabulary

## Actions in the Past

1. **belonged**

2. **depended**

3. **supported**

4. **borrowed**

5. **returned**

Score _____
(Top Score 5)

**Teacher** Read each word aloud. Have students trace the *-ed* suffix in each word.

| Vocabulary List | | |
|---|---|---|
| | 3. grandfather | 7. support |
| | 4. child | 8. cousin |
| 1. belong | 5. members | 9. related |
| 2. parent | 6. grandmother | 10. depend |

"Family" Vocabulary • Build New Vocabulary

## Word Play

## Yes or No?

1. Is a child related to his or her grandmother?    Yes    No

2. Is a child older than his or her grandfather?    Yes    No

3. Can you depend on a baby to take care of you?    Yes    No

4. Can a cousin also be a parent?    Yes    No

5. Can a family member support another family member?    Yes    No

**Teacher** Read each question aloud. Have students draw a circle around *Yes* if the question answers something that is possible or a circle around *No* if the question answers something that is impossible.

Score _____
(Top Score 5)

# "Good" Vocabulary

 **Word Meanings**

## Demonstrate

1. greet

 ○     ○

2. glad

 ○     ○

3. prize

 ○     ○

4. behave

 ○     ○

5. thank

 ○     ○

Score _____
(Top Score 5)

**Teacher** Read each word aloud. Have students fill in the bubble below the picture that best demonstrates the meaning of the word.

| Vocabulary List | 3. obey | 7. deserve |
|---|---|---|
| 1. behave | 4. glad | 8. promise |
| 2. thank | 5. prize | 9. greet |
|  | 6. blessing | 10. polite |

## 2 Reference Skills

# Dictionary Definitions

1. greet       ○ to be thankful       ○ to say hello

2. blessing    ○ something that        ○ something that
                 brings you              makes you sleepy
                 happiness

3. polite      ○ unkind               ○ kind and
                                         thoughtful

4. deserve     ○ to be worthy of;     ○ to act properly
                 to earn

5. promise     ○ to say good-bye      ○ to give your word
                                         that you will do
                                         something

**Teacher** Read each word and the definitions aloud
Have students fill in the bubble next to the correct
definition of the word.

Score _____
(Top Score 5)

## 3 Build New Vocabulary

# Context Clues

1. I made a _____ to my mom to clean my room, and I did it.
   promise    polite

2. We _____ our friends by saying, "Hello."
   greet    glad

3. I am _____ when my family eats together.
   behave    glad

4. We _____ people when they do something nice for us.
   thank    deserve

5. You might win a _____ at the fair.
   obey    prize

Score _____
(Top Score 5)

**Teacher** Tell students to listen carefully as you read each incomplete sentence aloud. Have them decide which word best completes the sentence and draw a circle around it.

| Vocabulary List | | |
|---|---|---|
| 1. behave | 3. obey | 7. deserve |
| 2. thank | 4. glad | 8. promise |
| | 5. prize | 9. greet |
| | 6. blessing | 10. polite |

"Good" Vocabulary • Build New Vocabulary

## Word Play

## Rhyming Words

1. What word rhymes with *greet* and means "parts of the body on which a person stands or walks"?

eet

2. What word rhymes with *glad* and means "angry"?

ad

3. What word rhymes with *prize* and means "the bigness of something"?

ize

4. What word rhymes with *thank* and means "a thing that holds money"?

ank

**Teacher** Read each riddle aloud. Have students write in the correct beginning letter to answer each rhyming riddle.

Score _____
(Top Score 4)

# Vocabulary Review

**1** Review Word Meanings

1. The children sat in a <u>circle</u> for storytime.

     ○         ○         ○

2. I turned the <u>page</u> in the book.

     ○         ○         ○

3. She tried to <u>guess</u> the right answer.

     ○         ○         ○

4. She wanted to <u>speak</u> to the teacher.

     ○         ○         ○

5. He would only take a <u>minute</u> to tie his shoe.

     ○         ○         ○

Score _____
(Top Score 5)

**Teacher** Read aloud the story on page 22 in the
*Teacher's Edition* OR read the sentences above for
each number. Tell students to fill in the bubble below
the picture that best matches the underlined word.

## ② Review Word Meanings

1. I like to <u>study</u> in my room.

○                      ○                      ○

2. He wrote me a letter on the <u>paper</u>.

○                      ○                      ○

3. She had to <u>return</u> the book.

○                      ○                      ○

4. Mario carries a blue-and-red <u>backpack</u>.

○                       ○                       ○

5. I brush my teeth <u>daily</u>.

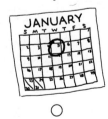    
○                       ○                       ○

**Teacher** Read aloud the story on page 23 in the *Teacher's Edition* OR read the sentences above for each number. Tell students to fill in the bubble below the picture that best matches the underlined word.

Score _____
(Top Score 5)

## 3 Review Word Meanings

1. There are five <u>members</u> in my family.

 ○     ○     ○

2. My <u>grandmother</u> came to visit yesterday.

 ○     ○     ○

3. His <u>grandfather</u> takes him fishing.

 ○     ○     ○

4. The <u>child</u> played in the sand.

 ○     ○     ○

5. One day I hope to be a <u>parent</u>.

 ○     ○     ○

Score _____
(Top Score 5)

**Teacher** Read aloud the story on page 24 in the *Teacher's Edition* OR read the sentences above for each number. Tell students to fill in the bubble below the picture that best matches the underlined word.

# 4    Review Word Meanings

1. <u>Dawn</u> is my favorite time of day.

   ○        ○        ○

2. I was <u>glad</u> to return home.

   ○        ○        ○

3. She received a <u>prize</u> for the best drawing.

   ○        ○        ○

4. I like to <u>greet</u> my dad at the bus stop.

   ○        ○        ○

5. I wrote a letter to <u>thank</u> Jean for the gift.

   ○        ○        ○

**Teacher** Read aloud the story on page 25 in the *Teacher's Edition* OR read the sentences above for each number. Tell students to fill in the bubble below the picture that best matches the underlined word.

Score _____
(Top Score 5)

# Vocabulary for Animals

**1** **Word Meanings**

## Who Am I?

1. bee                A.

2. bird               B.

3. cat                C.

4. cow                D.

5. duck               E.

6. dog                F.

7. fish               G.

8. fly                H.

9. frog               I.

10. horse             J.

Score _____
(Top Score 10)

**Teacher** Read each word aloud. Have students draw a line from the vocabulary word to its matching picture.

| Vocabulary List | | |
|---|---|---|
| 1. cat | 3. horse | 7. bee |
| 2. dog | 4. duck | 8. fish |
| | 5. fly | 9. frog |
| | 6. bird | 10. cow |

## 2 Reference Skills

# Dictionary Definitions

1. A **bee** makes honey.

A.

2. A **cat** has fur.

B.

3. A **duck** has wings.

C.

4. A **cow** gives milk.

D.

5. A **dog** can bark.

E.

**Teacher** Read each definition sentence aloud. Have students draw a line from the sentence to its matching picture.

Score _____
(Top Score 5)

# 3 Build New Vocabulary

## Kinds of Animals

1. dog

2. cat

3. fish

4. bird

5. duck

Score _____
(Top Score 5)

**Teacher** Read each word aloud. Have students draw an X over the picture that does NOT belong.

| Vocabulary List | | |
|---|---|---|
| 1. cat | 3. horse | 7. bee |
| 2. dog | 4. duck | 8. fish |
| | 5. fly | 9. frog |
| | 6. bird | 10. cow |

Vocabulary for Animals • Build New Vocabulary

 **Word Play**

## Baby Animals

1. sheep

**A.** kitten

2. cat

**B.** foal

3. cow

**C.** lamb

4. dog

**D.** pup

5. horse

**E.** calf

**Teacher** Read each word aloud. Have students draw a line from the animal name to the picture of its young.

Score _____
(Top Score 5)

# "Folktales" Vocabulary

## 1  Word Meanings

### Definitions

1. mouth

2. music

3. north

4. tale

5. folks

A. a pleasing combination of sounds

B. a story

C. people

D. opposite of south

E. part of the body that contains a tongue, teeth, and gums

Score _____
(Top Score 5)

**Teacher** Read each word aloud. Have students draw a line from the vocabulary word to its matching picture and definition.

| Vocabulary List | | |
|---|---|---|
| | 3. music | 7. mouth |
| | 4. live | 8. tale |
| 1. east | 5. south | 9. folks |
| 2. west | 6. north | 10. singer |

**Reference Skills**

## Guide Words

1. drop        good
   ○ east
   ○ west

2. lion        pat
   ○ north
   ○ tale

3. quiet       tame
   ○ folks
   ○ singer

4. minute      past
   ○ east
   ○ mouth

5. thank       win
   ○ west
   ○ music

6. rich        violet
   ○ singer
   ○ west

7. lemon       mop
   ○ live
   ○ mouth

8. snail       trim
   ○ singer
   ○ tale

9. until       yellow
   ○ south
   ○ west

10. eye        found
    ○ east
    ○ folks

**Teacher** Read each pair of guide words aloud. Have students fill in the bubble next to the word that would appear between the two guide words.

Score _____
(Top Score 10)

# 3 Build New Vocabulary

## Adding -er

1. teacher

2. reader

3. thinker

4. painter

5. player

Score _____
(Top Score 5)

**Teacher** Read each word aloud. Have students trace the -er ending in each word.

| Vocabulary List | | |
|---|---|---|
| 1. east | 3. music | 7. mouth |
| 2. west | 4. live | 8. tale |
| | 5. south | 9. folks |
| | 6. north | 10. singer |

"Folktales" Vocabulary • Build New Vocabulary

## Word Play

# Matching Related Words

1. live

2. see

3. sing

4. tell

5. think

A. thought

B. tale

C. life

D. sight

E. song

Score _____
(Top Score 5)

# The Circus

## Picture Definitions

**1. clown**

○       ○

**2. elephant**

○       ○

**3. lion**

○       ○

**4. tiger**

○       ○

**5. tent**

○       ○

Score _____
(Top Score 5)

**Teacher** Read each word aloud. Have students fill in the bubble below the picture that matches the word.

| Vocabulary List | | |
|---|---|---|
| 1. tame | 3. lion | 7. crowd |
| 2. clown | 4. tent | 8. hoop |
| | 5. elephant | 9. ticket |
| | 6. tiger | 10. show |

## ② Reference Skills

# Dictionary Sentences

1. A **lion** can roar.

A.

2. You need a **ticket** to see the show.

B.

3. The **clown** did funny tricks.

C.

4. A **tiger** is a big cat.

D.

5. The biggest land animal is an **elephant.**

E.

**Teacher** Read each sentence aloud. Have students draw a line from the sentence to its matching picture.

Score _____
(Top Score 5)

### ③ Build New Vocabulary

## More Than One

# At the circus,

# I saw two

# elephants, three

# tame lions, four

# clowns, five tents,

# and six tickets.

# Now I have been

# to two shows.

Score _____
(Top Score 6)

**Teacher** Read each sentence aloud. Have students trace the *-s* in each sentence.

| Vocabulary List | 3. lion | 7. crowd |
|---|---|---|
| 1. tame | 4. tent | 8. hoop |
| 2. clown | 5. elephant | 9. ticket |
| | 6. tiger | 10. show |

The Circus • Build New Vocabulary

# Word Play

## Grouping Words

1. hoop

2. clown           **People**

3. ticket

4. lion

                                        **Things**

5. crowd

6. tiger

7. tent

                                        **Animals**

8. elephant

**Teacher** Have students draw a line from the picture on the left to the word it can be categorized with on the right.

Score _____
(Top Score 8)

# Vocabulary for Sounds

**1** **Word Meanings**

## Let's Hear It

1. chirp

A.

2. croak

B.

3. roar

C.

4. squeal

D.

5. quack

E.

Score _____
(Top Score 5)

**Teacher** Read each word aloud. Have students draw a line from the word to the animal that makes the sound.

| Vocabulary List | 3. chirp | 7. hum |
|---|---|---|
| 1. quack | 4. groan | 8. roar |
| 2. squeal | 5. chatter | 9. giggle |
| | 6. whisper | 10. croak |

Vocabulary for Sounds • Word Meanings

## Reference Skills

# Dictionary Definitions

1. to talk quietly
   ○ whisper
   ○ squeal

2. a silly laugh
   ○ croak
   ○ giggle

3. a deep, sad sound
   ○ groan
   ○ chatter

4. to sing with a closed mouth
   ○ hum
   ○ chirp

5. fast, silly talk
   ○ quack
   ○ chatter

6. flat sound a duck makes
   ○ chirp
   ○ quack

7. a loud, deep sound
   ○ whisper
   ○ roar

8. deep, grating sound a frog makes
   ○ squeal
   ○ croak

9. a short, sharp sound
   ○ roar
   ○ chirp

10. a loud, high-pitched cry
    ○ squeal
    ○ hum

**Teacher** Read each definition aloud. Have students fill in the bubble of the word that matches the definition.

Score _____
(Top Score 10)

### 3 Build New Vocabulary

## Adding -ing

1. The lion is roaring.

2. The pig is squealing.

3. The birds are chirping.

4. The frog is croaking.

5. The ducks are quacking.

Score _____
(Top Score 5)

**Teacher** Read each sentence aloud. Have students trace the -ing ending in each sentence.

| Vocabulary List | 3. chirp | 7. hum |
|---|---|---|
| | 4. groan | 8. roar |
| 1. quack | 5. chatter | 9. giggle |
| 2. squeal | 6. whisper | 10. croak |

Vocabulary for Sounds • Build New Vocabulary

## Word Play

## Nonsense Rhymes

1. An eel does not _____ when it steals a meal.
   ○ squeal
   ○ croak

2. My thumb went numb, so I started to _____.
   ○ hum
   ○ giggle

3. Do you moan and _____ when you pick up a stone?
   ○ chirp
   ○ groan

4. The floor at the store makes a snore and a _____.
   ○ roar
   ○ croak

5. "Egg yolks make me choke," I spoke with a _____.
   ○ groan
   ○ croak

**Teacher** Read each nonsense rhyme aloud. Have students fill in the bubble next to the word that completes the nonsense rhyme.

Score _____
(Top Score 5)

# Vocabulary for Amounts

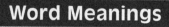

## ① Word Meanings

## Definitions

1. **batch:** an amount baked at one time; a group

2. **bundle:** a number of things tied or bound together

3. **dozen:** a group of twelve

4. **equal:** the same in size or number

5. **double:** two of the same thing

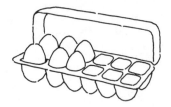

Score _____
(Top Score 5)

**Teacher** Read each word and definition aloud. Have students draw a circle around the picture that best matches the word and definition.

| Vocabulary List | 3. heap | 7. double |
|---|---|---|
| 1. equal | 4. batch | 8. bunch |
| 2. bundle | 5. dozen | 9. enough |
| | 6. exact | 10. bushel |

## Reference Skills

# Guide Words

1. baby     crow
   ○ batch
   ○ heap

2. day     dream
   ○ equal
   ○ dozen

3. end     fly
   ○ bunch
   ○ enough

4. hay     ink
   ○ heap
   ○ bundle

5. date     draw
   ○ exact
   ○ double

6. broad     butter
   ○ heap
   ○ bushel

7. age     canary
   ○ bunch
   ○ exact

8. dirt     evening
   ○ equal
   ○ batch

9. draw     flower
   ○ bushel
   ○ exact

10. bread     dog
    ○ bundle
    ○ enough

**Teacher** Read each pair of guide words aloud. Have students fill in the bubble next to the word that would appear between the two guide words.

Score _____
(Top Score 10)

## 3 Build New Vocabulary

## Context Clues

1. a _____ eggs
   ○ double      ○ dozen

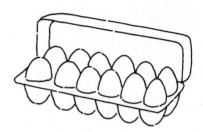

2. a _____ of biscuits
   ○ bushel      ○ batch

3. a _____ of apples
   ○ exact       ○ bushel

4. a _____ of newspapers
   ○ bundle      ○ enough

5. a _____ of bananas
   ○ bunch       ○ heap

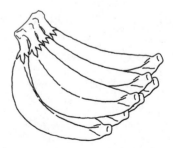

Score _____
(Top Score 5)

**Teacher** Read each phrase aloud. Have students fill in the bubble next to the word that best completes the phrase.

| Vocabulary List | 3. heap | 7. double |
|---|---|---|
| 1. equal | 4. batch | 8. bunch |
| 2. bundle | 5. dozen | 9. enough |
| | 6. exact | 10. bushel |

Vocabulary for Amounts • Build New Vocabulary

## Word Play

# Word Search

| batch | bunch | bundle |
| bushel | double | dozen | enough |
| equal | exact | heap |

| b | a | b | u | n | d | l | e | e | d | e | l | e |
|---|---|---|---|---|---|---|---|---|---|---|---|---|
| u | e | a | d | d | o | u | b | n | e | q | e | b |
| l | x | t | u | o | z | e | u | o | x | u | l | u |
| c | c | c | n | h | e | a | p | u | a | a | l | n |
| b | u | h | e | e | n | e | x | g | c | l | e | c |
| u | b | u | s | h | e | l | d | h | t | l | d | h |
| l | e | b | e | d | o | u | b | l | e | z | l | e |
| x | q | o | o | n | h | e | s | z | e | c | h | l |

**Teacher** Have students complete the word search by drawing a circle around each vocabulary word from the word box. Remind them that words are found going across and going down.

Score _____
(Top Score 10)

# Vocabulary Review

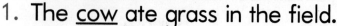

**1** **Review Word Meanings**

1. The <u>cow</u> ate grass in the field.

○            ○            ○

2. The <u>horse</u> trotted into the barn.

○            ○            ○

3. The <u>frog</u> hopped into the pond.

○            ○            ○

4. The <u>duck</u> quickly swam to the shore.

○            ○            ○

5. The <u>fish</u> would not swim near the hook.

○            ○            ○

Score _____
(Top Score 5)

**Teacher** Read aloud the story on page 46 in the *Teacher's Edition* OR read the sentences above for each number. Tell students to fill in the bubble below the picture that best matches the underlined word.

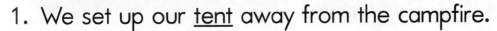

## ② Review Word Meanings

1. We set up our <u>tent</u> away from the campfire.

 ○      ○      ○

2. I bought a <u>ticket</u> to the circus.

 ○      ○      ○

3. The <u>clown</u> had a big red nose.

 ○      ○      ○

4. The <u>elephant</u> ate the whole bucket of peanuts.

 ○      ○      ○

5. The lion roared as he jumped through the <u>hoop</u>.

 ○      ○     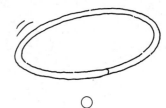 ○

**Teacher** Read aloud the story on page 47 in the *Teaohor's Edition* OR read the sentences above for each number. Tell students to fill in the bubble below the picture that best matches the underlined word.

Score _____
(Top Score 5)

Vocabulary Review           Unit 2 • Lesson 12    **47**

Lesson 12

## 3 Review Word Meanings

1. I could hear the bird <u>chirp</u> in the tree.

　　○　　　　　　○　　　　　　○

2. The frog let out a <u>croak</u> after he ate the fly.

　　○　　　　　　○　　　　　　○

3. When the ducks wanted more corn, they would <u>quack</u>.

　　○　　　　　　○　　　　　　○

4. We heard a loud <u>squeal</u> from the pigpen.

　　○　　　　　　○　　　　　　○

5. From behind the chair, Mother could hear a <u>giggle</u>.

　　○　　　　　　○　　　　　　○

Score _____
(Top Score 5)

**Teacher** Read aloud the story on page 48 in the *Teacher's Edition* OR read the sentences above for each number. Tell students to fill in the bubble below the picture that best matches the underlined word.

 **Review Word Meanings**

1. The grocer ordered a <u>bushel</u> of apples.

  ○    ○

2. Aunt Maria sold her <u>batch</u> of biscuits at the bake sale.

  ○    ○

3. Every Sunday Uncle Jack would buy a <u>dozen</u> roses.

  ○    ○

4. The farmer gathered a <u>heap</u> of grain.

  ○  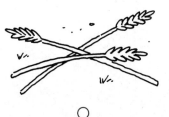  ○

5. The boys gathered a <u>bundle</u> of sticks for the campfire.

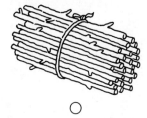  ○  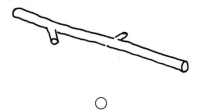  ○

**Teacher** Read aloud the story on page 49 in the *Teacher's Edition* OR read the sentences above for each number. Tell students to fill in the bubble below the picture that best matches the underlined word.

Score _____
(Top Score 5)

# "Things That Go" Vocabulary

**1** **Word Meanings**

## Picture Definitions

1. canoe

A.

2. train

B.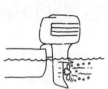

3. airplane

C.

4. motor

D.

5. carriage

E.

6. bicycle

F.

7. scooter

G.

8. tractor

H.

Score _____
(Top Score 8)

**Teacher** Read each word aloud. Have students draw a line from the vocabulary word on the left to the picture it matches on the right.

| Vocabulary List | | |
|---|---|---|
| 1. bicycle | 3. canoe | 7. train |
| 2. skateboard | 4. tractor | 8. airplane |
| | 5. cart | 9. scooter |
| | 6. motor | 10. carriage |

"Things That Go" Vocabulary • Word Meanings

## ② Reference Skills
## Alphabetical Order

_____ scooter

_____ skateboard

_____ airplane

_____ train

_____ bicycle

_____ motor

**Teacher** Read each word aloud. Using the numbers 1–6, have students place the words in alphabetical order by placing a 1 next to the word that would come first, 2 next to the word that would come second, and so on.

Score _____
(Top Score 6)

"Things That Go" Vocabulary • Reference Skills

# 3 Build New Vocabulary

## Compound Words

1. mail

2. air plane

3. skate board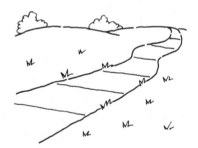

4. side walk

5. sail boat

Score _____
(Top Score 5)

**Teacher** Read each word aloud. Have students trace the smaller word to make the compound word that matches the picture.

| Vocabulary List | | |
|---|---|---|
| 1. bicycle | 3. canoe | 7. train |
| 2. skateboard | 4. tractor | 8. airplane |
| | 5. cart | 9. scooter |
| | 6. motor | 10. carriage |

"Things That Go" Vocabulary • Build New Vocabulary

## Word Play

### Rhyming Words

# train

track                bank                rain

cane                date                plane

- - - - - - - - - - - - - - - - - - - - - - - - - - - - - -

# cart

pin                dart                tan

part                heart                ran

**Teacher** Read each word aloud. Have students draw a circle around the words that rhyme with the words *train* and *cart*.

Score _____
(Top Score 6)

# Our Neighborhood at Work

**①**  **Word Meanings**

## People and Places

1. building

2. operator

**People**

3. lifeguard

4. factory

**Places**

5. plumber

6. clerk

Score _____
(Top Score 6)

**Teacher** Read each word aloud. Have students draw a line from the picture of the vocabulary word to the correct category.

| Vocabulary List | 3. clerk | 7. uniform |
|---|---|---|
| 1. building | 4. factory | 8. operator |
| 2. police | 5. handmade | 9. plumber |
|  | 6. office | 10. lifeguard |

Our Neighborhood at Work • **Word Meanings**

## Reference Skills

# Dictionary Sentences

1. A **clerk** works in a store.

**A.**

2. Goods are made in a **factory.**

**B.**

3. A **plumber** fixes water pipes.

**C.**

4. An **office** is a room to work in.

**D.**

5. The policewoman wears a **uniform** when she is on duty.

**E.**

**Teacher** Read each sentence aloud. Have students draw a line from the sentence to the picture it matches.

Score _____
(Top Score 5)

## 3 Build New Vocabulary

### Base Words

1.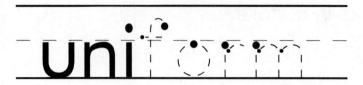
uniform

2.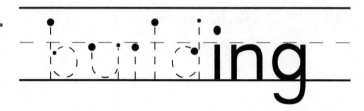
building

3.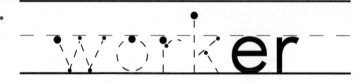
worker

4.
bicycle

5.
unequal

Score _____
(Top Score 5)

**Teacher** Have students trace
the base word in each word.

| Vocabulary List | | |
|---|---|---|
| 1. building | 3. clerk | 7. uniform |
| 2. police | 4. factory | 8. operator |
| | 5. handmade | 9. plumber |
| | 6. office | 10. lifeguard |

## Word Play

## The Missing Vowels

| | | | |
|---|---|---|---|
| building | lifeguard | clerk | factory |
| handmade | office | operator | plumber |
| police | uniform | | |

1. b___ld_ng

2. l_f_g___rd

3. _p_r_t_r

4. pl__mb__r

5. h_ndm_d_

**Teacher** Read each word in the box aloud.
Have the students write in the missing vowels
in each word.

Score _____
(Top Score 16)

# Places to Live

**1** **Word Meanings**

## Animal and People Homes

1. cabin   cage

2. cave   cottage

3. coop   wigwam

4. hut   den

5. igloo   nest

Score _____
(Top Score 5)

**Teacher** Read each pair of words aloud. Have students look at each pair of pictures and then circle the word that represents where people live.

| Vocabulary List | 3. wigwam | 7. igloo |
|---|---|---|
| 1. nest | 4. coop | 8. cottage |
| 2. cabin | 5. hut | 9. cave |
| | 6. den | 10. cage |

# 2 Reference Skills

## Guide Words

1. cabin
   ○ bank/early          ○ glad/jump

2. cage
   ○ bank/early          ○ glad/jump

3. hut
   ○ bank/early          ○ glad/jump

4. den
   ○ bank/early          ○ glad/jump

5. igloo
   ○ bank/early          ○ glad/jump

**Teacher** Read each word aloud. Have students fill in the bubble next to the set of guide words each vocabulary word would be found between.

Score _____
(Top Score 5)

## 3 Build New Vocabulary

# Context Clues

1. We paddled the **canoe** down the river.

A.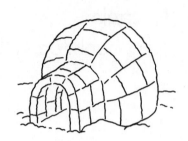

2. Although it was made of ice, the **igloo** was warm inside.

B.

3. We wore **moccasins** on our feet.

C.

4. A **raccoon** has mask-like markings on its face and a bushy, ringed tail.

D.

5. We picked the **tomato** from the plant.

E.

Score _____
(Top Score 5)

**Teacher** Read each sentence aloud. Have students draw a line from the sentence to the picture it matches.

| Vocabulary List | 3. wigwam | 7. igloo |
|---|---|---|
| 1. nest | 4. coop | 8. cottage |
| 2. cabin | 5. hut | 9. cave |
| | 6. den | 10. cage |

Places to Live • Build New Vocabulary

 **Word Play**

# What Is It Made Of?

1. cabin

**A.** ice

2. cage

**B.** twigs and leaves

3. hut

**C.** thatch

4. igloo

**D.** wire

5. nest

**E.** wood

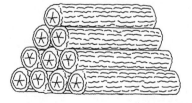

**Teacher** Read each word aloud. Have students draw a line from the word to the picture of the material usually used to build that home. Have students refer to the pictures on page 58 for help.

Score _____
(Top Score 5)

# Vocabulary for Making Faces
## 1 Word Meanings

### Demonstrate

1. grin

A.

2. frown

B.

3. mask

C.

4. wink

D.

5. yawn

E.

Score _____
(Top Score 5)

**Teacher** Read each word aloud. Have students draw a line from the word to the picture it matches.

| Vocabulary List | 3. smile | 7. blink |
|---|---|---|
| | 4. blush | 8. surprise |
| 1. mask | 5. yawn | 9. pretend |
| 2. frown | 6. wink | 10. grin |

## Reference Skills

# Beginning, Middle, End

1. blush
   ○ A–H          ○ I–Q          ○ R–Z

2. pretend
   ○ A–H          ○ I–Q          ○ R–Z

3. mask
   ○ A–H          ○ I–Q          ○ R–Z

4. wink
   ○ A–H          ○ I–Q          ○ R–Z

5. frown
   ○ A–H          ○ I–Q          ○ R–Z

6. surprise
   ○ A–H          ○ I–Q          ○ R–Z

**Teacher** Read each word aloud. Have students fill in the bubble next to the letters that tell where the word can be found in a dictionary.

Score _____
(Top Score 6)

## Build New Vocabulary

## Add *-ing*

1. Why do you keep blink_____ your eyes?

2. I am blush_____ because I am shy.

3. Luis is frown_____ in that picture.

4. Tora is pretend_____ to be sad.

5. My doll looks as if she is wink_____ at me.

6. Josh cannot stop yawn_____ today.

Score _____
(Top Score 6)

**Teacher** Read each sentence aloud. Have students trace the *-ing* at the end of the vocabulary words.

| Vocabulary List | | |
|---|---|---|
| 1. mask | 3. smile | 7. blink |
| 2. frown | 4. blush | 8. surprise |
| | 5. yawn | 9. pretend |
| | 6. wink | 10. grin |

Vocabulary for Making Faces • Build New Vocabulary

## Word Play

## Related Words

1. grin
   - ○ smile
   - ○ frown

2. wink
   - ○ blush
   - ○ blink

3. mask
   - ○ pretend
   - ○ yawn

4. yawn
   - ○ wink
   - ○ sleepy

5. giggle
   - ○ laugh
   - ○ blink

6. blush
   - ○ red
   - ○ blue

7. surprise
   - ○ slowly
   - ○ suddenly

8. frown
   - ○ joyful
   - ○ unhappy

**Teacher** Read each word aloud. Have students fill in the bubble next to the word that best relates to the vocabulary word.

Score _____
(Top Score 8)

# Describing People

## 1 Word Meanings

### Synonyms

1. silly     mad     angry

2. beautiful     handsome     ugly

3. shy     truthful     honest

4. angry     silly     funny

5. sleepy     lucky     drowsy

6. pretty     beautiful     gentle

Score _____
(Top Score 6)

**Teacher** Read each word aloud. Have students draw an X over the word that is NOT a synonym.

| Vocabulary List | |
| --- | --- |
| 1. shy | 3. gentle |
| 2. beautiful | 4. drowsy |
| | 5. silly |
| | 6. lucky |

| | |
| --- | --- |
| 7. handsome | |
| 8. honest | |
| 9. angry | |
| 10. nice | |

## ② Reference Skills

## How Many Syllables?

1. _____

**angry**

2. _____

**beautiful**

3. _____

**honest**

4. _____

**gentle**

5. _____

**nice**

**Teacher** Read each word aloud. Count the number of syllables in each word with the students. Then have the students write the number on the line provided.

Score _____
(Top Score 5)

## 3 Build New Vocabulary

## The Suffix -ful

1. The meadow was beauti_____.

2. Pedro was very help_____.

3. The kittens are play_____.

4. It was a rest_____ afternoon.

5. Leo is care_____ when he is

crossing the street.

Score _____
(Top Score 5)

**Teacher** Have students trace the -ful at the end of the vocabulary words to make the sentence match the picture.

| Vocabulary List | 3. gentle | 7. handsome |
|---|---|---|
| | 4. drowsy | 8. honest |
| 1. shy | 5. silly | 9. angry |
| 2. beautiful | 6. lucky | 10. nice |

## Word Play

# Animal Rhymes

1. shy

A.

2. nice

B.

3. slow

C.

4. fake

D.

5. that

E.

**Teacher** Read each word aloud. Have students draw a line from the word to the picture of the animal that it rhymes with.

Score _____
(Top Score 5)

# Vocabulary Review

**1** **Review Word Meanings**

1. The <u>airplane</u> flew from New York to Texas.

    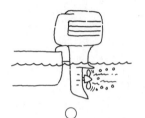

○    ○    ○

2. Luisa pedaled the <u>bicycle</u> up the hill.

○    ○    ○

3. The <u>train</u> chugged slowly up the mountain.

○    ○    ○

4. Mom and I paddled the <u>canoe</u> down the river.

○    ○    ○

5. The farmer plowed the field with the <u>tractor</u>.

○    ○    ○

Score _____
(Top Score 5)

**Teacher** Read aloud the story on page 70 in the *Teacher's Edition* OR read the sentences for each number. Tell students to fill in the bubble below the picture that best matches the underlined word.

## ② Review Word Meanings

1. We watched the people make cars at the <u>factory</u>.

○                      ○                      ○

2. Uncle Martin wears a tie when he works in the <u>office</u>.

○                      ○                      ○

3. The <u>police</u> officer gave us directions to the park.

○                      ○                      ○

4. The <u>operator</u> wore her safety goggles.

○                       ○                       ○

5. The <u>plumber</u> used his wrench to fix the pipe.

○                       ○                       ○

**Teacher** Read aloud the story on page 71 in the *Teacher's Edition* OR read the sentences for each number. Tell students to fill in the bubble below the picture that best matches the underlined word.

Score _____
(Top Score 5)

## 3 Review Word Meanings

1. Soto used bark and leaves to build the <u>wigwam</u>.

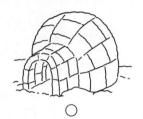        

   ◯            ◯            ◯

2. The family huddled together inside the <u>igloo</u>.

    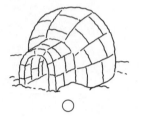    

   ◯            ◯            ◯

3. Mother told us to come into the <u>hut</u> to get away from the hot sun.

   ◯            ◯            ◯

4. The bat rested in the <u>cave</u> during the day.

   ◯            ◯            ◯

5. The bluebird brought food back to her <u>nest</u>.

   ◯            ◯            ◯

Score _____
(Top Score 5)

**Teacher** Read aloud the story on page 72 in the *Teacher's Edition* OR read the sentences for each number. Tell students to fill in the bubble below the picture that best matches the underlined word.

**Review Word Meanings**

1. Would you <u>frown</u> at a clown?

2. Peter was <u>angry</u> that he had to wait for his turn.

3. Talking in front of a lot of people always makes me <u>blush</u>.

4. We all laughed at the <u>silly</u> clowns.

5. The cat was <u>lucky</u> that the firefighter rescued it.

**Teacher** Read aloud the story on page 73 in the *Teacher's Edition* OR read the sentences for each number. Tell students to fill in the bubble below the picture that best matches the underlined word.

Score _____
(Top Score 5)

# "Weather" Vocabulary

**1**     Word Meanings

## What's the Picture?

1. cloud

                 **A.**

2. frost

                 **B.**

3. rainbow

                 **C.**

4. sunny

                 **D.**

5. tornado

                 **E.**

6. snowfall

                 **F.**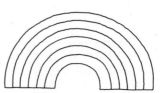

Score _____
(Top Score 6)

**Teacher** Read each word aloud. Have students draw a line from the vocabulary word on the left to its matching picture on the right.

| Vocabulary List | 3. sunny | 7. rainbow |
|---|---|---|
| 1. rain | 4. cloud | 8. tornado |
| 2. frost | 5. fog | 9. snowfall |
| | 6. hurricane | 10. thunder |

## ② Reference Skills

## Number of Syllables

1. _____  sunny

2. _____  rain

3. _____  thunder

4. _____  hurricane

5. _____  fog

6. _____  tornado

**Teacher** Have students count the number of syllables in each word. Tell them to write the number in the space provided.

Score _____
(Top Score 6)

## Build New Vocabulary

### Add -y

1. rain + y = _____

2. frost + y = _____

3. sun + n + y = _____

4. cloud + y = _____

5. snow + y = _____

Score _____
(Top Score 5)

**Teacher** Have students look at each equation. Instruct them to write the word on the line, adding -y to the letters as indicated.

| Vocabulary List | 3. sunny | 7. rainbow |
|---|---|---|
| | 4. cloud | 8. tornado |
| 1. rain | 5. fog | 9. snowfall |
| 2. frost | 6. hurricane | 10. thunder |

"Weather" Vocabulary • Build New Vocabulary

## Word Play

## Nonsense Rhymes

| rain | tornado | sunny | fog |
|------|---------|-------|-----|

_____

- - - - - - - - - - - - - -

1. A <u>frog</u> left its <u>log</u> to <u>jog</u> in the _____ .

_____

- - - - - - - - - - - - - -

2. On the way to <u>Spain</u>, I saw _____

   in the <u>plane</u>.

3. The <u>funny</u> bee makes <u>honey</u> only when it is

   _____

   - - - - - - - - - - - - - -

   _____ .

   _____

   - - - - - - - - - - - - - -

4. A _____ ! Oh, <u>no</u>! It will <u>blow</u>

   things that <u>grow</u>!

**Teacher** Read aloud each rhyme. Have students
write the word from the box that completes it. The
underlined words rhyme with the answer.

Score _____
(Top Score 4)

# Machines in Our Garden
## 1  Word Meanings

## Picture Definitions

| ax | hole | seed | shovel | weed |

1.

_____

- - - - - - - - - - - - -

_____

2.

_____

- - - - - - - - - - - - -

_____

3.

_____

- - - - - - - - - - - - -

_____

4.

_____

- - - - - - - - - - - - -

_____

5.

_____

- - - - - - - - - - - - -

_____

Score _____
(Top Score 5)

**Teacher** Have students look at each picture and write the word from the box that matches on the line provided.

| Vocabulary | 3. ax | 7. seed |
| List | 4. plow | 8. hole |
| 1. shovel | 5. weed | 9. field |
| 2. wheelbarrow | 6. soil | 10. fill |

## ② Reference Skills

# More Than One Meaning

1. plow

2. shovel

 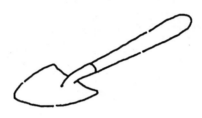 

3. weed

4. field

 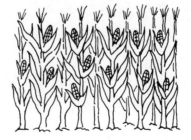 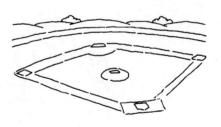

**Teacher** Read each word aloud. Have students draw an X over the picture that does not match the meaning of the word.

Score _____
(Top Score 4)

# ③ Build New Vocabulary

## Words That Sound Alike

1. 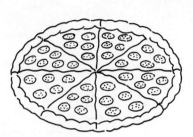 ○ hole    ○ whole

2.  ○ ate    ○ eight

3.  ○ sea    ○ see

4.  ○ tale    ○ tail

5.  ○ son    ○ sun

Score _____
(Top Score 5)

**Teacher** Read each word choice aloud. Have students darken the oval next to the word that matches the picture.

| Vocabulary List | | |
|---|---|---|
| | 3. ax | 7. seed |
| | 4. plow | 8. hole |
| 1. shovel | 5. weed | 9. field |
| 2. wheelbarrow | 6. soil | 10. fill |

## Word Play

# Can You?

1. Can a farmer plow a field?

_____
- - - - - - - - - - - - -
_____

2. Can soil shovel an ax?

_____
- - - - - - - - - - - - -
_____

3. Can you put a seed in a hole?

_____
- - - - - - - - - - - - -
_____

4. Can an ax shovel a wheelbarrow?

_____
- - - - - - - - - - - - -
_____

5. Can you fill a hole?

_____
- - - - - - - - - - - - -
_____

6. Can a gardener pull a weed from the soil?

_____
- - - - - - - - - - - - -
_____

**Teacher** Read each question aloud. Have students write the word *yes* or *no* to answer the question correctly.

Score _____
(Top Score 6)

# "Earth" Vocabulary

## Word Meanings

## Definitions

| ash | cliff | forest | island | tip |
|-----|-------|--------|--------|-----|

1. _____

the end point of something

2. _____

a small area of land surrounded by water

3. _____

gray powder left by something that has been burned

4. _____

an area of land covered with trees and other plants

5. _____

a high, steep wall of rock

Score _____
(Top Score 5)

**Teacher** Read each definition aloud. Have students write the word from the box that matches the definition.

| Vocabulary List | 3. forest | 7. prairie |
|-----------------|-----------|------------|
| 1. ash | 4. cliff | 8. tip |
| 2. canyon | 5. island | 9. valley |
| | 6. nature | 10. mountain |

## 2 Reference Skills

# Alphabetical Order by Second Letter

1. _____ fruit      _____ forest

2. _____ plant      _____ prairie

3. _____ nest      _____ nature

4. _____ volcano      _____ valley

5. _____ cliff      _____ canyon

**Teacher** Read each set of words aloud. Have students write *1* next to the word that would come first in alphabetical order and *2* next to the word that would come next.

Score \_\_\_\_\_
(Top Score 5)

## Build New Vocabulary

# Context Clues: Spanish Words

1. I like to eat a crunchy <u>taco</u>.

2. They sat on the <u>patio</u> and enjoyed the sun.

3. We rode a donkey into the deep <u>canyon</u>.

4. The <u>alligator</u> came out of the water to rest.

5. The <u>mosquito</u> landed on my arm.

Score _____
(Top Score 5)

**Teacher** Read each sentence aloud. Have students draw a line from the sentence to the picture that matches the underlined word.

| Vocabulary List | | |
|---|---|---|
| 1. ash | 3. forest | 7. prairie |
| 2. canyon | 4. cliff | 8. tip |
| | 5. island | 9. valley |
| | 6. nature | 10. mountain |

"Earth" Vocabulary • Build New Vocabulary

## Word Play

## Missing Consonants

| ash | forest | island | mountain | nature |
|-----|--------|--------|----------|--------|

1.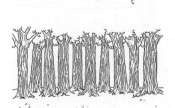

   __ o __ e __ __

2.

   __ ou __ __ ai __

3.

   i __ __ a __ __

4.

   __ a __ u __ e

5.

   a __ __

**Teacher** Have students look at each picture and provide the missing consonants for each word. Have students use the words in the box for reference.

Score _____
(Top Score 17)

# "Water" Vocabulary

## 1 Word Meanings

### Answering Questions

1. Can you fill a glass with a drop of dew?                    yes                    no

2. If your toy boat has a leak, will it still float?                    yes                    no

3. If a river is overflowing, is it getting smaller or larger?                    smaller                    larger

4. Can a whale live in a puddle?                    yes                    no

5. Which is larger—a lake or an ocean?                    lake                    ocean

Score _____
(Top Score 5)

**Teacher** Read each question and the two answer choices aloud. Have students circle the correct answer.

| Vocabulary List | | |
|---|---|---|
| 1. river | 3. lake | 7. float |
| 2. ocean | 4. ice | 8. hose |
| | 5. puddle | 9. leak |
| | 6. dew | 10. overflow |

## ② Reference Skills

## Dictionary Sentences

1. Drops of <u>dew</u> form on flowers.

2. Turn on the <u>hose</u> and water the garden.

3. A raft is used to <u>float</u> on water.

4. Evan splashed in the <u>puddle</u>.

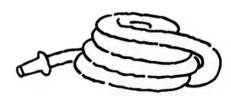

5. <u>Ice</u> is frozen water.

**Teacher** Read each sentence aloud. Have students draw a line from the dictionary sentence to the picture that best represents the underlined word.

Score _____
(Top Score 5)

## 3 Build New Vocabulary

## Compound Words

1. ice water

2. dewdrop

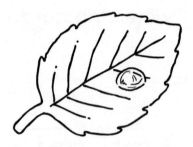

3. riverboat

4. riverside

Score _____
(Top Score 4)

**Teacher** Read each word aloud. Have students draw a line from the compound word to the picture that matches.

| Vocabulary List | 3. lake | 7. float |
|---|---|---|
| 1. river | 4. ice | 8. hose |
| 2. ocean | 5. puddle | 9. leak |
| | 6. dew | 10. overflow |

"Water" Vocabulary • Build New Vocabulary

## Word Play

## Rhyming Words

1. I would think <u>twice</u> about chewing on

   _____

   - - - - - - - - - - - - - - - - - -

   _____ .

2. The lettuce <u>grows</u> if you water it with the

   _____

   - - - - - - - - - - - - - - - - - -

   _____ .

3. Claire made the <u>mistake</u> of taking her <u>snake</u> to the

   _____

   - - - - - - - - - - - - - - - - - -

   _____ .

4. Our coach asked us to <u>huddle</u> next to the

   _____

   - - - - - - - - - - - - - - - - - -

   _____ .

5. Did you <u>sneak</u> a <u>peak</u> at the

   _____

   - - - - - - - - - - - - - - - - - -

   _____ ?

**Teacher** Read each sentence aloud. Have students write the vocabulary word that rhymes with each underlined word. Have students refer to vocabulary words that are displayed in the classroom.

Score _____
(Top Score 5)

# "Bad Behavior" Vocabulary

**1**  **Word Meanings**

## Words That Mean the Same

| grab | greedy | nasty | slap | tease |

1. **snatch:** to grasp suddenly or quickly

   _____

   - - - - - - - - - - - - - - - - -

   _____

2. **mean:** not nice; unkind

   _____

   - - - - - - - - - - - - - - - - -

   _____

3. **smack:** to hit

   _____

   - - - - - - - - - - - - - - - - -

   _____

4. **selfish:** wanting things only for yourself

   _____

   - - - - - - - - - - - - - - - - -

   _____

5. **mock:** to make fun of

   _____

   - - - - - - - - - - - - - - - - -

   _____

Score _____
(Top Score 5)

**Teacher** Read each word aloud. Have students write the vocabulary word from the box that means the same as the word that is shown.

| Vocabulary List | | |
|---|---|---|
| 1. blame | 3. wicked | 7. mean |
| 2. slap | 4. cheat | 8. nasty |
| | 5. grab | 9. pest |
| | 6. greedy | 10. tease |

## Reference Skills

## Glossary Sentences

| pest | blame | Wicked | cheat | mean |
|------|-------|--------|-------|------|

_____

1. We _____ our dog for the muddy floor.

_____

2. You are _____ to tease that dog.

_____

3. We do not _____ when we play games.

_____

4. _____ people are not kind.

_____

5. A _____ is something that bothers you.

**Teacher** Read each incomplete sentence aloud to students.
Have students use their glossary to look up each word in
the word box. Then have students write the correct
vocabulary word on the line in each sentence.

Score _____
(Top Score 5)

"Bad Behavior" Vocabulary • Reference Skills

## Build New Vocabulary

## Good and Bad

| | | | | |
|---|---|---|---|---|
| cheat | wicked | helpful | kind | obey |
| cruel | gentle | greedy | nasty | share |

### Good Behavior

_____

- - - - - - - - - - - - - -

_____

- - - - - - - - - - - - - -

_____

- - - - - - - - - - - - - -

_____

- - - - - - - - - - - - - -

_____

- - - - - - - - - - - - - -

_____

### Bad Behavior

_____

- - - - - - - - - - - - - -

_____

- - - - - - - - - - - - - -

_____

- - - - - - - - - - - - - -

_____

- - - - - - - - - - - - - -

_____

- - - - - - - - - - - - - -

_____

Score _____
(Top Score 10)

**Teacher** Read each word aloud. Have students write each word from the box in the *Good Behavior* or the *Bad Behavior* category.

| Vocabulary List | | |
|---|---|---|
| 1. blame | 3. wicked | 7. mean |
| 2. slap | 4. cheat | 8. nasty |
| | 5. grab | 9. pest |
| | 6. greedy | 10. tease |

"Bad Behavior" Vocabulary • Build New Vocabulary

## Word Play

## Rhyming Clues

| blame | cheat | greedy | pest | slap |
|-------|-------|--------|------|------|

1. _____ to <u>beat</u> by not playing fair

2. _____ to hit with a sound like a <u>clap</u>

3. _____ an unwanted <u>guest</u>

4. _____ to <u>shame</u>

5. _____ <u>needy</u> in a selfish way

**Teacher** Read each rhyming clue aloud. Have students write the word from the box that matches the definition and rhymes with the underlined word.

Score _____
(Top Score 5)

# Vocabulary Review

**1** **Review Word Meanings**

1. There were no people on the small <u>island</u>.

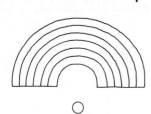      

   ○        ○        ○

2. The winds from the <u>hurricane</u> knocked over the tree.

   ○        ○        ○

3. The basement is a safe place to go during a <u>tornado</u>.

   ○        ○        ○

4. The weatherman said there would be heavy <u>snowfall</u>.

   ○        ○        ○

5. The sun set behind the <u>mountain</u>.

   ○        ○        ○

Score _____
(Top Score 5)

**Teacher** Read aloud the story on page 94 in the *Teacher's Edition* OR read the numbered sentences. Tell students to fill in the bubble below the picture that best matches the underlined word.

## ② Review Word Meanings

1. The river flowed right through the <u>valley</u>.

 ◯      ◯      ◯

2. The tractor pulled the <u>plow</u> over the field.

 ◯      ◯      ◯

3. Rosa planted her <u>seed</u> in the garden.

 ◯      ◯      ◯

4. Raymond used a <u>shovel</u> to dig a large hole.

     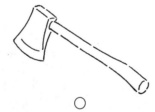     
 ◯      ◯      ◯

5. Then he used the <u>wheelbarrow</u> to haul away the dirt.

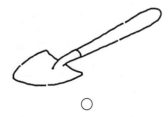     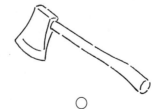     
 ◯      ◯      ◯

**Teacher** Read aloud the story on page 95 in the
*Teacher's Edition* OR read the numbered sentences.
Tell students to fill in the bubble below the picture
that best matches the underlined word.

Score _____
(Top Score 5)

## 3 Review Word Meanings

1. The fox ran into the <u>forest</u>.

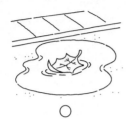 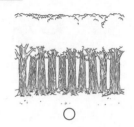 

2. The flower petals were wet from the morning <u>dew</u>.

3. Frogs were jumping in the <u>puddle</u>.

 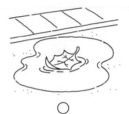 

4. She used the raft to <u>float</u> in the pool.

5. The mountain goat stood at the edge of the <u>cliff</u>.

  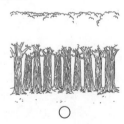

Score _____
(Top Score 5)

**Teacher** Read aloud the story on page 96 in the
*Teacher's Edition* OR read the numbered sentences.
Tell students to fill in the bubble below the picture
that best matches the underlined word.

Vocabulary Review

 **Review Word Meanings**

1. The <u>greedy</u> man kept all the candy to himself.
   ○ nice      ○ angry      ○ selfish

2. We are not allowed to <u>slap</u> anyone at school.
   ○ smack      ○ silly      ○ pest

3. She said she would <u>grab</u> the toy from me if I did not give it to her.
   ○ blame      ○ snatch      ○ mean

4. Brian's mom told him not to <u>tease</u> his little sister.
   ○ slap      ○ plow      ○ mock

5. Everyone thought that the bully was <u>mean</u>.
   ○ unkind      ○ nice      ○ greedy

**Teacher** Read aloud the story on page 97 in the *Teacher's Edition* OR read the numbered sentences. Tell students to fill in the bubble next to the word that means the same as the underlined word.

Score _____
(Top Score 5)

# "Journeys" Vocabulary

## 1  Word Meanings

### Definitions

| arrive | baggage | mile | prepare | travel |
|--------|---------|------|---------|--------|

1. to get ready

   _____
   - - - - - - - - - - - - -
   _____

2. to go on a trip

   _____
   - - - - - - - - - - - - -
   _____

3. to get to a place

   _____
   - - - - - - - - - - - - -
   _____

4. a unit of length that equals 5,280 feet

   _____
   - - - - - - - - - - - - -
   _____

5. bags to carry things in

   _____
   - - - - - - - - - - - - -
   _____

Score _____
(Top Score 5)

**Teacher** Read each word aloud. Have students write the vocabulary word from the box that matches the definition.

| Vocabulary List | 3. baggage | 7. mile |
|-----------------|------------|---------|
| | 4. travel | 8. passenger |
| 1. rough | 5. tour | 9. prepare |
| 2. arrive | 6. sink | 10. rest |

## Reference Skills

# More Than One Meaning

1. sink

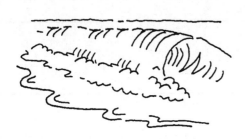   

| rest | sink | tour |

2. Mom says to put the dirty dishes in the

_____

– – – – – – – – – – – –

_____ .

_____

– – – – – – – – – – –

3. After taking a _____ of the ship, the

_____

– – – – – – – – – – – – – –

passengers wanted to sit down and _____ .

**Teacher** For the top part read the word *sink* aloud. Then have students circle the pictures that represent the two different meanings of *sink*. For the bottom part have students write the correct word from the word box in the blank. Each word is used once.

Score _____
(Top Score 5)

## ③ Build New Vocabulary

## Irregular Past Tense

| fell | flew | ran | threw | wrote |
|------|------|-----|-------|-------|

1. throw

2. write

3. run

4. fall

5. fly

Score _____
(Top Score 5)

**Teacher** Read each word aloud. Tell students to choose the irregular past tense of the word from the words in the box. Have them write the word they chose next to the matching picture.

| Vocabulary List | 3. baggage | 7. mile |
|-----------------|------------|---------|
| 1. rough | 4. travel | 8. passenger |
| 2. arrive | 5. tour | 9. prepare |
| | 6. sink | 10. rest |

"Journeys" Vocabulary • Build New Vocabulary

## Changing Letters

| c | g | k | p | w |
|---|---|---|---|---|

1. <u>r</u>ough

_____

- - - - - - - - - - - - - - -

_____

2. mil<u>e</u>

_____

- - - - - - - - - - - - - - -

_____

3. <u>s</u>ink

_____

- - - - - - - - - - - - - - -

_____

4. sin<u>k</u>

_____

- - - - - - - - - - - - - - -

_____

5. <u>t</u>our

_____

- - - - - - - - - - - - - - -

_____

**Teacher** Read each word aloud. Have students identify the underlined letter in each word. Have students create new words by replacing the underlined letter with a letter from the box. Have them write the new word that matches the picture in the blank.

Score _____
(Top Score 5)

# "Keep Trying" Vocabulary

**1**  **Word Meanings**

## Synonyms

1. back          forward          advance

2. gift          game          contest

3. effort          stop          try

4. gain          win          lose

5. glory          honor          repeat

6. adjust          change          begin

Score _____
(Top Score 6)

**Teacher** Read each set of words aloud. Have students draw an X over the word that does not mean the same as the other two words.

| Vocabulary List | 3. advance | 7. contest |
|---|---|---|
| 1. adjust | 4. gain | 8. effort |
| 2. champion | 5. glory | 9. almost |
|  | 6. repeat | 10. finally |

"Keep Trying" Vocabulary • Word Meanings

## Reference Skills

# Which Comes First?

1. almost     advance

_____
- - - - - - - - - - - - - - - - - - - - -
_____

2. champion    contest

_____
- - - - - - - - - - - - - - - - - - - - -
_____

3. glory        gain

_____
- - - - - - - - - - - - - - - - - - - - -
_____

4. finally      forest

_____
- - - - - - - - - - - - - - - - - - - - -
_____

5. effort      engine

_____
- - - - - - - - - - - - - - - - - - - - -
_____

**Teacher** Read each pair of words aloud. Have students underline the second letter in each word. Then have them write the word that would come first alphabetically in the blank.

Score _____
(Top Score 15)

 **Build New Vocabulary**

## The Prefix *re-*

| rebuild | refill | rewrite | reread | repaint |

1. _____

2. _____

3. _____

4. _____

5. _____

Score _____
(Top Score 5)

**Teacher** Read each word in the box aloud. Have students write each word next to its matching picture.

| Vocabulary List | 3. advance | 7. contest |
|---|---|---|
| 1. adjust | 4. gain | 8. effort |
| 2. champion | 5. glory | 9. almost |
| | 6. repeat | 10. finally |

"Keep Trying" Vocabulary • Build New Vocabulary

## Word Play

## How Many Words?

# champion

_____

- - - - - - - - - - - - - - - - - -

_____

- - - - - - - - - - - - - - - - - -

_____

- - - - - - - - - - - - - - - - - -

_____

- - - - - - - - - - - - - - - - - -

_____

- - - - - - - - - - - - - - - - - -

_____

**Teacher** Have students create five new words from the letters of the word *champion* and write them in the blanks.

Score _____
(Top Score 5)

"Keep Trying" Vocabulary • Word Play

# "Shapes and Sizes" Vocabulary

## 1  Word Meanings

### Picture Definitions

| curve | giant | heavy | straight | tiny |
| --- | --- | --- | --- | --- |

1. _____

2. _____

3. _____

4. _____

5. _____

Score _____
(Top Score 5)

**Teacher** Read the words in the box aloud. Have students write each word next to its matching picture.

| Vocabulary List | 3. wide | 7. thin |
| --- | --- | --- |
| 1. bent | 4. spiral | 8. curve |
| 2. giant | 5. heavy | 9. tiny |
| | 6. straight | 10. flat |

# Reference Skills

## Using a Glossary

| bent | flat | giant | spiral | wide |
|------|------|-------|--------|------|

1. The _____ mountain was very tall.

2. He gently _____ the tree branch.

3. The _____ stairs curved around to the second floor.

4. No one could jump across the _____ river.

5. A piece of paper is very _____.

Score _____
(Top Score 5)

# 3 Build New Vocabulary

## Antonyms

| narrow | straight | light | big | thick |
|---|---|---|---|---|

1. thin

_____
- - - - - - - - - - - - -
_____

2. tiny

_____
- - - - - - - - - - - - -
_____

3. wide

_____
- - - - - - - - - - - - -
_____

4. bent

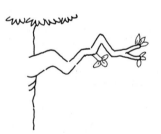

_____
- - - - - - - - - - - - -
_____

5. heavy

_____
- - - - - - - - - - - - -
_____

Score _____
(Top Score 5)

**Teacher** Read each word in the box aloud. Have students write each word next to the word and picture that have the opposite meaning.

| Vocabulary List | | |
|---|---|---|
| 1. bent | 3. wide | 7. thin |
| 2. giant | 4. spiral | 8. curve |
| | 5. heavy | 9. tiny |
| | 6. straight | 10. flat |

"Shapes and Sizes" Vocabulary • Build New Vocabulary

# Word Play

## Similes

| flat | heavy | tiny | wide |
|------|-------|------|------|

1. I was so tired that my eyelids seemed as

   _____

   - - - - - - - - - - - - - -

   _____ as a rock.

2. My baseball cap was as

   _____

   - - - - - - - - - - - - - -

   _____ as a pancake

   after the car rolled over it.

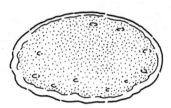

3. Your smile is as _____

   as the ocean.

4. My little brother looked as

   _____

   - - - - - - - - - - - - - -

   _____ as an ant next

   to the tall basketball player.

**Teacher** Read each word aloud. Have students complete each simile by writing a word from the box in the blank. Tell them to use the pictures for help.

Score _____
(Top Score 4)

# Going to the Doctor's Office

**1  Word Meanings**

## How Do You Feel?

| accident | fever | heal | medicine | scratch |
|---|---|---|---|---|

1.

2.

3.

4.

5.

**Teacher** Read the words in the box aloud. Have students write each word next to its matching picture.

| Vocabulary List | 3. ache | 7. medicine |
|---|---|---|
| | 4. fever | 8. harm |
| 1. accident | 5. scratch | 9. shiver |
| 2. heal | 6. pain | 10. pale |

## Reference Skills

# Which Is Correct?

1. aksident      accident      accedent

2. ache      ake      ach

3. feever      fevere      fever

4. haerm      harm      harme

5. shiver      chiver      shever

**Teacher** Read each word aloud. Have students draw a circle around the correct spelling of the word. They may use their glossaries for help.

Score _____
(Top Score 5)

## 3 Build New Vocabulary

## Context Clues: Homophones

| heal | heel | pail | pale |
|------|------|------|------|

1. He could not get the sock over his

   _____

   - - - - - - - - - -

   _____.

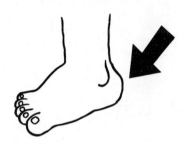

2. She carried the water home in a

   _____

   - - - - - - - - - -

   _____.

3. After seeing the scary movie, his face

   _____

   - - - - - - - - - -

   turned _____.

4. The doctor said that rest would help

   _____

   - - - - - - - - - -

   _____ her broken leg.

Score _____
(Top Score 4)

**Teacher** Read each word in the box and each sentence aloud. Have students complete each sentence with the correct word from the box.

| Vocabulary List | 3. ache | 7. medicine |
|---|---|---|
| | 4. fever | 8. harm |
| 1. accident | 5. scratch | 9. shiver |
| 2. heal | 6. pain | 10. pale |

Going to the Doctor's Office • Build New Vocabulary

# Word Play

## Scrambled Words

1. mahr

_____

- - - - - - - - - - - - -

_____

to cause pain

2. elap

_____

- - - - - - - - - - - - -

_____

having a white color; lacking color

3. verhis

_____

- - - - - - - - - - - - -

_____

to shake

4. chea

_____

- - - - - - - - - - - - -

_____

to be in constant pain

5. leha

_____

- - - - - - - - - - - - -

_____

to get well

6. inpa

_____

- - - - - - - - - - - - -

_____

a feeling of hurt

**Teacher** Tell students to unscramble each set of letters to form a vocabulary word. Have them write the word in the blank. Encourage them to use the definition hints for help.

Score _____
(Top Score 6)

# Prepositions

**1**   Word Meanings

## Examples

| above | outside | through | on |
|---|---|---|---|

———————————————————
- - - - - - - - - - - - - - - - - - -

1. The bird is ——————————————

   its cage.

———————————————————
- - - - - - - - - - - - - - - - - - -

2. It flew ——————————————

   the window.

3. Then the bird landed

———————————————————
- - - - - - - - - - - - - - - - - - -

   ———————————————— the roof.

———————————————————
- - - - - - - - - - - - - - - - - - -

4. It flew high ——————————————

   the house.

**Teacher** Read the words in the box and the sentences aloud. Tell students to look at each picture. Have them complete each sentence using a word from the box.

| Vocabulary List | 3. inside | 7. below |
|---|---|---|
| | 4. without | 8. among |
| 1. on | 5. outside | 9. beyond |
| 2. along | 6. above | 10. through |

Prepositions • Word Meanings

## 2 Reference Skills

# Alphabetize By Second Letter

| around | among | above | across | along |
|--------|-------|-------|--------|-------|

| Letter | Word |
|--------|------|
| 1. _____ | _____ |
| 2. _____ | _____ |
| 3. _____ | _____ |
| 4. _____ | _____ |
| 5. _____ | _____ |

**Teacher** Read each word from the box aloud. Have students write the second letter of each word in alphabetical order in the blanks under the *Letter* column. Then have them write the word that goes with each letter in the *Word* column.

Prepositions • Reference Skills

Score _____
(Top Score 10)

**Build New Vocabulary**

## *Up* and *Out*

| outfield | outfit | outgrow | uphill | upstairs |
| --- | --- | --- | --- | --- |

1. He put on his mitt as he ran into the

_____

\_ \_ \_ \_ \_ \_ \_ \_ \_ \_ \_ \_ \_ \_ \_ \_ \_ \_ \_

_____ to play baseball.

_____

\_ \_ \_ \_ \_ \_ \_ \_ \_ \_ \_ \_ \_ \_ \_ \_ \_ \_ \_

2. All the bedrooms were _____.

_____

\_ \_ \_ \_ \_ \_ \_ \_ \_ \_ \_ \_ \_ \_ \_ \_ \_ \_ \_

3. It is hard to pedal a bike _____.

_____

\_ \_ \_ \_ \_ \_ \_ \_ \_ \_ \_ \_ \_ \_ \_ \_ \_ \_ \_

4. She decided to wear the red _____.

_____

\_ \_ \_ \_ \_ \_ \_ \_ \_ \_ \_ \_ \_ \_ \_ \_ \_ \_ \_

5. Soon the baby will _____ these tiny

clothes.

Score _____
(Top Score 5)

**Teacher** Read the words from the box and the sentences aloud. Have students complete each sentence with the correct compound word from the box.

| **Vocabulary List** | 3. inside | 7. below |
| --- | --- | --- |
| 1. on | 4. without | 8. among |
| 2. along | 5. outside | 9. beyond |
| | 6. above | 10. through |

# Word Play

## A or Be?

| a | be |
|---|---|

_____

- - - - - - - -

1. under        _____low

_____

- - - - - - - -

2. over         _____bove

_____

- - - - - - - -

3. over the length of   _____long

_____

- - - - - - - -

4. gone         _____way

_____

- - - - - - - -

5. at an earlier time   _____fore

**Teacher** Read each short definition aloud. Have students complete the word that matches the definition by writing *a* or *be* in the blank.

Score _____
(Top Score 5)

# Vocabulary Review

 **Review Word Meanings**

1. Carlos liked to <u>travel</u> by bicycle.
   - ○ to fall to the bottom
   - ○ to take a trip
   - ○ to get ready

2. Alicia chose some books to <u>prepare</u> for the long bus ride.
   - ○ to take a trip
   - ○ to get ready
   - ○ to get to a place

3. Raul liked being a <u>passenger</u> on the boat.
   - ○ moving water
   - ○ a person who rides in a boat, airplane, or car
   - ○ suitcases and bags

4. The plane had to go to Chicago before it could <u>arrive</u> in New York.
   - ○ to get ready
   - ○ to take a trip
   - ○ to get to a place

5. Thankfully it would not be a <u>rough</u> trip.
   - ○ easy
   - ○ sandpaper
   - ○ difficult

Score _____
(Top Score 5)

**Teacher** Read aloud the story on page 118 in the *Teacher's Edition* OR read the numbered sentences. Tell students to fill in the bubble next to the definition that matches the underlined word.

## Review Word Meanings

1. Eli was excited to win the <u>contest</u>.
   - ○ a game
   - ○ a try
   - ○ a winner

2. Marta had to <u>adjust</u> her glasses so she could see better.
   - ○ to do again
   - ○ to try
   - ○ to rearrange

3. It took a lot of <u>effort</u>, but we finally won the game.
   - ○ a game
   - ○ a winner
   - ○ a try

4. My little sister likes to <u>repeat</u> everything I say.
   - ○ to go forward
   - ○ to do again
   - ○ to win

5. Vince was considered to be a <u>champion</u> on the soccer field.
   - ○ a game
   - ○ a try
   - ○ a winner

**Teacher** Read aloud the story on page 119 in the
*Teacher's Edition* OR read the numbered sentences.
Tell students to fill in the bubble next to the
definition that matches the underlined word.

Score _____

(Top Score 5)

 **Review Word Meanings**

1. The rock was too <u>heavy</u> to move.

    ○        ○        ○

2. The path went <u>straight</u> into the forest.

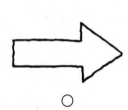    ○    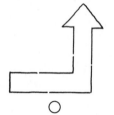    ○        ○

3. The bird was flying <u>through</u> the trees.

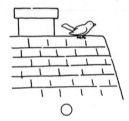    ○        ○        ○

4. The bus slowed down as it went around the <u>curve</u>.

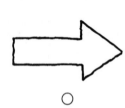    ○    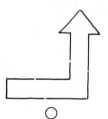    ○        ○

5. The bird flew high <u>above</u> the houses.

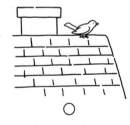    ○        ○        ○

Score _____
(Top Score 5)

**Teacher** Read aloud the story on page 120 in the *Teacher's Edition* OR read the numbered sentences. Tell students to fill in the bubble below the picture that best matches the underlined word.

 **Review Word Meanings**

1. The antenna on the television was <u>bent</u>.
   - ○ straight
   - ○ crooked
   - ○ flat

2. The cold wind made me <u>shiver</u>.
   - ○ shake
   - ○ ache
   - ○ pale

3. Pablo found a <u>scratch</u> on his knee.
   - ○ fever
   - ○ heal
   - ○ scrape

4. The water was <u>below</u> the bridge.
   - ○ under
   - ○ along
   - ○ beyond

5. Aunt Karen would not <u>harm</u> even a fly.
   - ○ heal
   - ○ hurt
   - ○ shiver

**Teacher** Read aloud the story on page 121 in the
*Teacher's Edition* OR read the numbered sentences.
Tell students to fill in the bubble next to the word
that means the same as the underlined word.

Score _____
(Top Score 5)

# "Being Afraid" Vocabulary

## 1    Word Meanings

### Examples

1. hide

○

○

2. alley

○

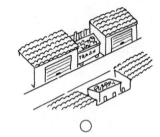
○

3. blanket

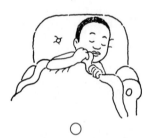
○

○

4. howl

○

○

5. smoke

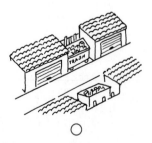
○

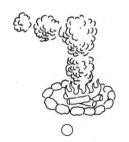
○

Score _____
(Top Score 5)

**Teacher** Read each word aloud. Have students fill in the bubble below the picture that best matches the word.

| Vocabulary List | | |
|---|---|---|
| 1. howl | 3. alarm | 7. smoke |
| 2. blanket | 4. hide | 8. nothing |
|  | 5. nightmare | 9. alley |
|  | 6. monster | 10. cover |

## 2 Reference Skills

# Dictionary Definitions

| alarm | monster | nightmare | nothing | cover |
|-------|---------|-----------|---------|-------|

1. a scary, made-up creature

_____

2. a warning of danger

_____

3. not any thing

_____

4. a bad dream

_____

5. to be over the surface of; to hide from view

_____

**Teacher** Read each definition aloud. Have students write the word from the box next to its correct definition.

Score _____
(Top Score 5)

## Build New Vocabulary

## Compound Words

| bowling alley | hideout | smoke alarm |
|---|---|---|
| alarm clock | smokestack | |

1.

2.

3.

4.

5.

**Teacher** Read each word aloud. Have students write each word from the box next to its matching picture.

| Vocabulary | 3. alarm | 7. smoke |
|---|---|---|
| List | 4. hide | 8. nothing |
| 1. howl | 5. nightmare | 9. alley |
| 2. blanket | 6. monster | 10. cover |

"Being Afraid" Vocabulary • Build New Vocabulary

 **Word Play**

## Silly Rhymes

| alley | howl | hide | nightmare | smoke |

1. <u>Sally</u> kept a <u>tally</u> for the ant race in the

_____

_ _ _ _ _ _ _ _ _ _ _ _ _ _ _ _ _

_____ .

_____

_ _ _ _ _ _ _ _ _ _ _ _ _ _ _ _ _

2. Did you see the elephants _____
<u>inside</u> from the mouse they <u>spied</u>?

3. The <u>bear</u> and <u>Claire</u> had the same

_____

_ _ _ _ _ _ _ _ _ _ _ _ _ _ _ _ _

_____ .

4. An <u>owl</u> on the <u>prowl</u> doesn't <u>growl</u> or

_____

_ _ _ _ _ _ _ _ _ _ _ _ _ _ _ _ _

_____ .

_____

_ _ _ _ _ _ _ _ _ _ _ _ _ _ _ _ _

5. I <u>awoke</u> to _____

coming from the <u>artichoke</u>.

**Teacher** Read each silly rhyme aloud. Have
students write the word from the box that best
completes each rhyme. (**HINT:** The word will rhyme
with the underlined word.)

Score _____
(Top Score 5)

# More Animals

## 1  Word Meanings

### Picture Definitions

1. _____

2. _____

3. _____

4. _____

5. _____

Score _____
(Top Score 5)

**Teacher** Have students write the correct animal name next to its picture.

| Vocabulary List | |  |
|---|---|---|
| 1. crab | 3. caterpillar | 7. butterfly |
| 2. chipmunk | 4. beaver | 8. turtle |
|  | 5. dove | 9. penguin |
|  | 6. ape | 10. rabbit |

More Animals • Word Meanings

## Reference Skills

# Guide Words

| beaver | butterfly | caterpillar | penguin | rabbit |

1. break/by

_____

2. pale/pot

_____

3. can/cave

_____

4. queen/rose

_____

5. back/box

_____

**Teacher** Read each pair of guide words aloud. Have students write each word from the box next to the guide words it can be found between.

Score _____
(Top Score 5)

## ③ Build New Vocabulary

# Animal Characteristics

| beaver | butterfly | crab | rabbit | turtle |
|---|---|---|---|---|

1. long ears

_____

2. pretty wings

_____

3. pinching claws

_____

4. can hide its head inside its shell

_____

5. strong teeth for gnawing on wood

_____

Score _____
(Top Score 5)

**Teacher** Read each animal characteristic aloud. Have students write each word from the box next to the characteristic that describes that animal.

| Vocabulary List | 3. caterpillar | 7. butterfly |
|---|---|---|
| | 4. beaver | 8. turtle |
| 1. crab | 5. dove | 9. penguin |
| 2. chipmunk | 6. ape | 10. rabbit |

## Word Play

# More Similes

| beaver | butterfly | rabbit | turtle |

1. Our old van moves as slowly as a

   _____

   - - - - - - - - - - -

   _____ .

   (has short legs and a curved shell)

2. Some goals are as hard to catch as a

   _____

   - - - - - - - - - - -

   _____ .

   (an insect)

3. My teacher says that I am as eager as a

   _____

   - - - - - - - - - - -

   _____ because I work so

   hard in school.

   (its tail looks like a paddle)

4. When it comes to eating dessert, my sister is as quick as a

   _____

   - - - - - - - - - - -

   _____ .

   (some of these have cotton tails)

**Teacher** Read each incomplete simile aloud. Have students write the word from the box that best completes the simile. Encourage them to use the hints for help.

Score _____
(Top Score 4)

# Parts of a House

## Word Meanings

**1**

### Describe It

| ceiling | stairs | roof | chimney | dining room |
|---------|--------|------|---------|-------------|

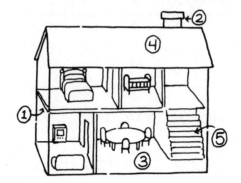

1. _____

2. _____

3. _____

4. _____

5. _____

Score _____
(Top Score 5)

**Teacher** Read the words from the box aloud. Have students write each word in the blank next to the correct location in the house.

| Vocabulary List | 3. dining room | 7. garage |
|-----------------|----------------|-----------|
| 1. ceiling | 4. nursery | 8. cupboard |
| 2. cellar | 5. roof | 9. porch |
| | 6. chimney | 10. stairs |

**Reference Skills**

# Alphabetical Order

| garage | dining room | porch | cupboard | nursery |
| --- | --- | --- | --- | --- |

1. couch

_____

- - - - - - - - - - - - - - - - - - - - - - -

2. _____

3. desk

_____

- - - - - - - - - - - - - - - - - - - - - - -

4. _____

5. fan

_____

- - - - - - - - - - - - - - - - - - - - - - -

6. _____

7. house

_____

- - - - - - - - - - - - - - - - - - - - - - -

8. _____

9. patio

_____

- - - - - - - - - - - - - - - - - - - - - - -

10. _____

11. railing

**Teacher** Read each word aloud. Have students complete the list by writing the words from the box in alphabetical order.

Score _____
(Top Score 5)

## Build New Vocabulary

## Words That Go Together

| cellar | chimney | cupboard | dining room | garage |

1. basement

_____

- - - - - - - - - - - - - - - - - - - - - - -

_____

2. shelf

_____

- - - - - - - - - - - - - - - - - - - - - - -

_____

3. driveway

_____

- - - - - - - - - - - - - - - - - - - - - - -

_____

4. table and chairs

_____

- - - - - - - - - - - - - - - - - - - - - - -

_____

5. fireplace

_____

- - - - - - - - - - - - - - - - - - - - - - -

_____

Score _____
(Top Score 5)

**Teacher** Read each word aloud. Have students write the word from the box next to its related word or words.

| Vocabulary List | | |
|---|---|---|
| 1. ceiling | 3. dining room | 7. garage |
| 2. cellar | 4. nursery | 8. cupboard |
| | 5. roof | 9. porch |
| | 6. chimney | 10. stairs |

**Word Play**

# Things That Go Together

| ceiling | dining room | garage | nursery | porch |
|---------|-------------|--------|---------|-------|

1.

2.

3.

4.

5.

**Teacher** Read the words from the box aloud. Have students write each word next to the picture that it best relates to.

Score _____
(Top Score 5)

# "Movement" Vocabulary

## 1 Word Meanings

### Demonstrate

| chase | grip | pass | throw | tumble |
|-------|------|------|-------|--------|

1. tip

2. race

3. jumble

4. go

5. grass

**Teacher** Read the words aloud. Have students write each word from the box next to its rhyming word and matching picture.

| Vocabulary List | 3. dodge | 7. grip |
|---|---|---|
| 1. dart | 4. drift | 8. throw |
| 2. pass | 5. tumble | 9. dash |
|  | 6. chase | 10. roll |

"Movement" Vocabulary • Word Meanings

## ② Reference Skills
## Glossary Sentences

| grip | dodge | pass | chase | drift |
|---|---|---|---|---|

_____

1. You should _____ the football to

another player.

_____

2. Try to _____ the ball and not get hit.

_____

3. Cats like to _____ mice.

_____

4. _____ the baseball bat with both hands.

_____

5. We let our boat _____ down the river.

**Teacher** Read each incomplete sentence aloud to students. Have them use their glossary to look up each word in the word box. Then have them write the correct vocabulary word on the line in each sentence.

Score \_\_\_\_\_
(Top Score 5)

## 3 Build New Vocabulary

# Context Clues

1. After he hit the ball with the club, we watched it <u>roll</u> into the hole.

  ○       ○       ○

2. Marc <u>dashed</u> across the ice to get to the puck.

  ○       ○       ○

3. The coach told me to <u>grip</u> the football tightly.

  ○       ○       ○

4. Anita wanted to <u>tumble</u> three times over the mat before doing a cartwheel.

  ○       ○       ○

5. The goalie <u>dodged</u> the ball at first, but Tammy still kicked it in to score a goal.

  ○       ○       ○

Score _____
(Top Score 5)

**Teacher** Read each sentence aloud. Have students fill in the bubble below the picture of the sport or game that the sentence describes.

| Vocabulary List | | |
|---|---|---|
| | 3. dodge | 7. grip |
| | 4. drift | 8. throw |
| 1. dart | 5. tumble | 9. dash |
| 2. pass | 6. chase | 10. roll |

# Crossword Puzzle

| carriage | cupboard | dodge | fog | pass |
| coop | dart | drift | grip | roll |

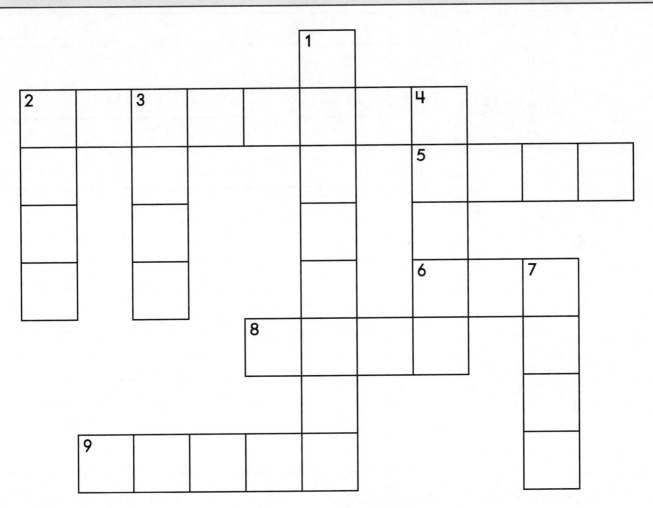

## Across

2. a place for dishes
5. turn over and over
6. thick mist
8. move quickly and suddenly
9. jump aside

## Down

1. a cart drawn by horses
2. home for a chicken
3. throw
4. float
7. hold tightly

**Teacher** Have students read each clue and then complete the crossword puzzle using the words from the box.

Score _____
(Top Score 10)

"Movement" Vocabulary • Word Play

Unit 6 • Lesson 34    **137**

# Useful Objects

## ① Word Meanings

### Examples

| basket | hook | knob | pot | toothbrush |

1.
   _____
   - - - - - - - - - - - - - - - - - - - -
   _____

2. 
   _____
   - - - - - - - - - - - - - - - - - - - -
   _____

3. 
   _____
   - - - - - - - - - - - - - - - - - - - -
   _____

4. 
   _____
   - - - - - - - - - - - - - - - - - - - -
   _____

5. 
   _____
   - - - - - - - - - - - - - - - - - - - -
   _____

Score _____
(Top Score 5)

**Teacher** Read the words in the box aloud. Have students write each word next to its matching picture.

| Vocabulary List | 3. rope | 7. rag |
|---|---|---|
| 1. hook | 4. thimble | 8. bowl |
| 2. knob | 5. toothbrush | 9. basket |
| | 6. pot | 10. dish |

Useful Objects • Word Meanings

## ② Reference Skills

# Dictionary Sentences

1. We eat soup from a <u>bowl</u>.

A.

2. A <u>rag</u> is used for cleaning.

B.

3. She wears a <u>thimble</u> while she sews.

C.

4. We used the <u>rope</u> to pull the boat to shore.

D.

5. Mom put the chicken on the <u>dish</u>.

E.

**Teacher** Read each sentence aloud. Have students draw a line from the sentence to its matching picture.

Score _____
(Top Score 5)

## Build New Vocabulary

## Useful Uses

| dish | hook | pot | rag | thimble |

1. cleaning _____

2. eating _____

3. sewing _____

4. cooking _____

5. hanging _____

Score _____
(Top Score 5)

**Teacher** Read each word aloud. Have students write the word from the box next to the word that best describes its use.

| Vocabulary List | | |
|---|---|---|
| 1. hook | 3. rope | 7. rag |
| 2. knob | 4. thimble | 8. bowl |
| | 5. toothbrush | 9. basket |
| | 6. pot | 10. dish |

## Word Play

# Rhymes

| bowl | dish | hook | pot | rope |
|------|------|------|-----|------|

_____

1. a <u>fish</u> on a _____

_____

2. <u>soap</u> on a _____

_____

3. a very <u>hot</u> _____

_____

4. a <u>hole</u> in a _____

_____

5. a _____ over a <u>brook</u>

**Teacher** Read each incomplete rhyme aloud. Have students write the word from the box that best completes the rhyme. (**Hint:** The underlined words rhyme with the correct word.)

Score _____
(Top Score 5)

# Vocabulary Review

## 1   Review Word Meanings

1. We watched the <u>penguin</u> dive into the water.

2. Even though the fire was out, he could still see <u>smoke</u>.

3. The baby slept quietly in the <u>nursery</u>.

4. The <u>ape</u> climbed the tree to reach the fruit.

5. Aunt Mae carried the eggs in her <u>basket</u>.

Score _____
(Top Score 5)

**Teacher** Read aloud the story on page 142 in the *Teacher's Edition* OR read the numbered sentences. Tell students to fill in the bubble below the picture that best matches the underlined word.

# 2 Review Word Meanings

1. Grandma likes to eat dinner in the <u>dining room</u>.

    ○              ○              ○

2. Juan stacked the plates in the <u>cupboard</u>.

          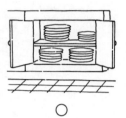

    ○              ○              ○

3. Aunt Maria planted a seed in the <u>pot</u>.

    ○              ○              ○

4. A <u>thimble</u> protects your finger when you sew.

    ○              ○              ○

5. The <u>caterpillar</u> made its chrysalis under the leaf.

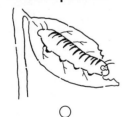          

    ○              ○              ○

**Teacher** Read aloud the story on page 143 in the *Teacher's Edition* OR read the numbered sentences. Tell students to fill in the bubble below the picture that best matches the underlined word.

Score _____
(Top Score 5)

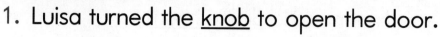

## Review Word Meanings

1. Luisa turned the <u>knob</u> to open the door.

      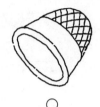

2. We watched the toy sailboat <u>drift</u> down the river.

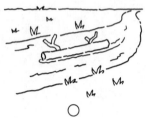      

3. Uncle Phil parked his car in the <u>garage</u>.

4. I hung my coat on the <u>hook</u>.

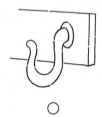      

5. Mom lets us <u>throw</u> pennies into the fountain.

      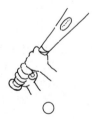

Score _____
(Top Score 5)

**Teacher** Read aloud the story on page 144 in the *Teacher's Edition* OR read the numbered sentences. Tell students to fill in the bubble below the picture that best matches the underlined word.

Vocabulary Review

 **Review Word Meanings**

## 1. Mother stored the old toys in the <u>cellar</u>.

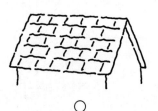   ○

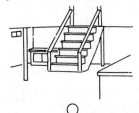   ○

   ○

## 2. We had to <u>grip</u> the rope to pull the boat to shore.

   ○

   ○

   ○

## 3. The <u>crab</u> walked across the sand.

   ○

   ○

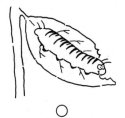   ○

## 4. Pedro used the <u>rope</u> to tie the stacks of newspaper.

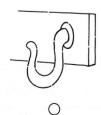   ○

   ○

   ○

## 5. The cat would <u>hide</u> whenever the dog came into the room.

   ○

   ○

   ○

**Teacher** Read aloud the story on page 145 in the *Teacher's Edition* OR read the numbered sentences. Tell students to fill in the bubble below the picture that best matches the underlined word.

Score _____
(Top Score 5)

# Cumulative Review

## Definitions

| backpack | nursery | sink | blush |
|----------|---------|------|-------|
| howl | music | finish | island |

1. You can carry your books in it

   _____

2. A small piece of land surrounded by water

   _____

3. A room for a baby

   _____

4. You can listen to this on the radio

   _____

5. A loud sound a wolf makes

   _____

6. If a boat has a leak, it will do this

   _____

Score _____
(Top Score 6)

**Teacher** Tell students to read each clue carefully. Then have them select the word from the box that best fits the clue and write it in the blank. Two words will not be used.

## Synonyms

1.    morning   night   dawn

2.    kick   throw   toss

3.    pile   heap   exact

4.    cottage   park   cabin

5.    tiny   giant   big

6.    ready   end   finish

**Teacher** Tell students to look carefully at each picture as you read each word choice aloud. Have them draw an X over the word that does NOT represent the picture.

Score _____
(Top Score 6)

## Sentence Completion

| Quack plumber | Polite crowd | crab giggle | cow |
|---|---|---|---|

_____

1. _____ people say "Please" and

"Thank you."

2. The _____ came to fix the

water pipes.

3. We saw a _____ walking on

the beach.

4. There was a big _____ of people

at the circus.

5. I heard the duck say, "_____."

Score _____
(Top Score 5)

**Teacher** Read each incomplete sentence aloud.
Have students select the word from the box
that best completes each sentence and write
it in the blank. Two words will not be used.

# Words and Themes

1.  factory        Useful Objects

2. 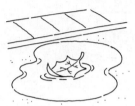 puddle        Movement

3.  bicycle        Things That Go

4.  rope        Water

5.  grandmother        Family

6.  tumble        Our Neighborhood at Work

**Teacher** Read each word and theme aloud. Tell students to draw a line from the word on the left to the correct theme on the right. Have them complete this exercise without looking back at the Vocabulary Lists in each lesson.

Score _____
(Top Score 6)

# Word Webs

You can draw a word web. A **word web** helps you think of words that are related.

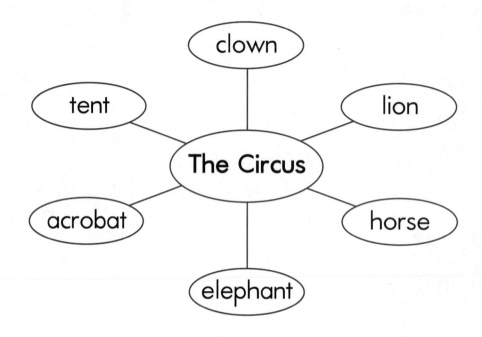

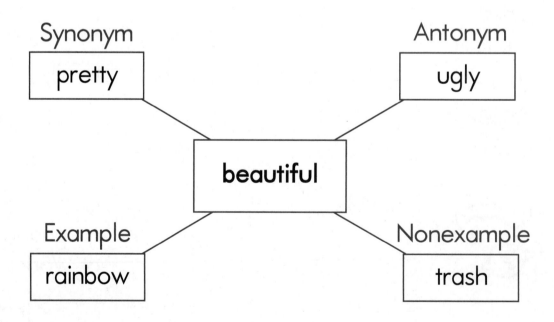

# Categorization

You can place words into categories, or groups.

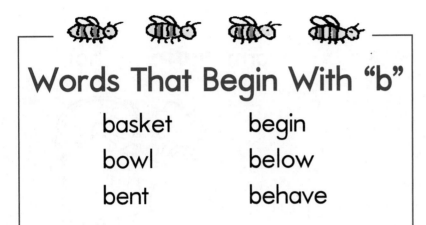

## Words That Begin With "b"

| | |
|---|---|
| basket | begin |
| bowl | below |
| bent | behave |

The words in each category have something in common.

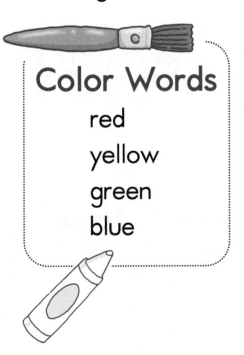

## Color Words
red
yellow
green
blue

## Animals
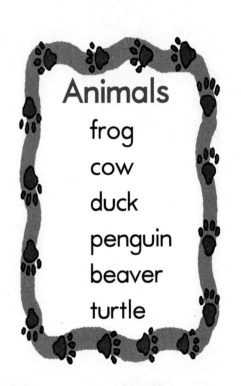
frog
cow
duck
penguin
beaver
turtle

## Weather Words

| | |
|---|---|
| rain | frost |
| snow | cloud |
| sunshine | thunder |

# Linear Graphs

A **linear graph** is another way to show how words are related.

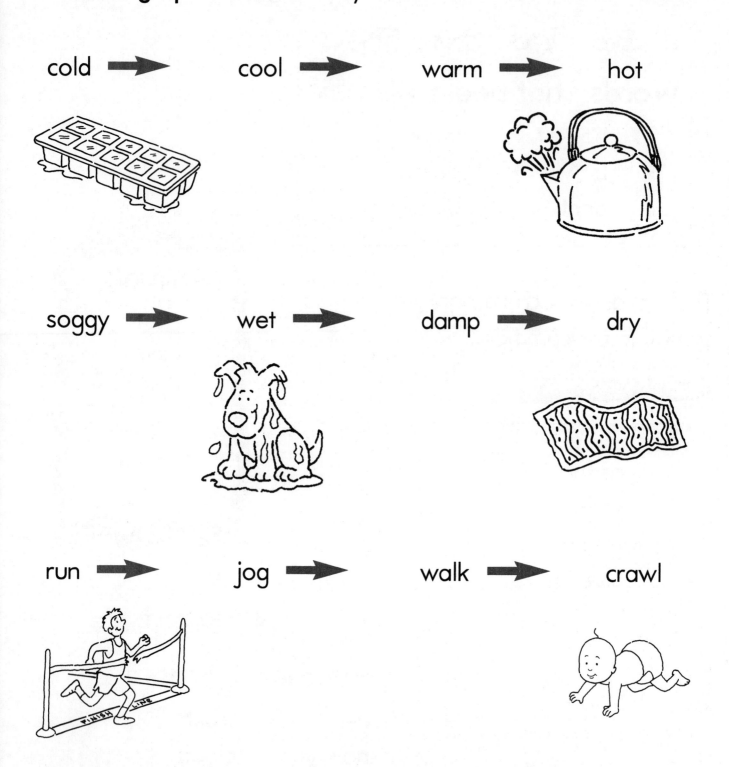

cold ➡ cool ➡ warm ➡ hot

soggy ➡ wet ➡ damp ➡ dry

run ➡ jog ➡ walk ➡ crawl

**Cool** is warmer than **cold**. **Warm** is cooler than **hot**.

# Context Clues

A **context clue** is a clue to the meaning of a word.

New Word

The dog likes to <u>chase</u> the cat.

Context Clue

*Chase* means "to run after something."

····························································································

New Word

The <u>tale</u>, "Jack and the Beanstalk," is a fun story to read.

Context Clue

*Tale* means "story."

# Context Clues

You can use context clues when you read. They help you learn more words.

The bus ride to the museum was long, but our visit was **brief.** We stayed at the museum for only one hour.

Can you see clues in the sentences that tell what *brief* means?

# How to Use Context Clues

1. Look at the sentence.
2. Point to the word or words you do not know.
3. Ask yourself, "Is the meaning of the word in the sentence?"
4. Ask yourself, "Is the opposite meaning of the word in the sentence?"
5. Look at the sentences before and after to find more clues.

# Word Relationships

**Antonyms** have opposite meanings.

## Antonyms

new/old                above/below

cool/warm              open/close

short/tall             push/pull

up/down                happy/sad

·····································································································

**Synonyms** have the same or about the same meanings.

## Synonyms

begin/start            crooked/bent

mad/angry              fast/quick

close/shut             old/ancient

end/finish             yell/shout

# Word Relationships

## Word Families

The words in a **word family** have some of the same sounds and letters in them.

### The *it* Word Family

| | | |
|---|---|---|
| it | bit | sit |
| kit | pit | wit |
| hit | fit | |

### The *all* Word Family

| | | |
|---|---|---|
| ball | stall | tall |
| call | small | wall |
| fall | hall | |

........................................................................................

## Homophones and Homographs

**Homophones** are words that sound the same but are not spelled the same. They have different meanings.

### Homophones

| | | |
|---|---|---|
| hare/hair | new/knew | sun/son |
| bare/bear | see/sea | two/to |

........................................................................................

**Homographs** are words that look the same but have different meanings.

### Homographs

| | |
|---|---|
| bat: a flying animal<br>bat: a club for hitting a<br>      baseball | wind: the air that blows<br>      outside<br>wind: to turn many times |

# BUILDING
# Vocabulary
## *Skills*

## Level 1
# Home Connection
### To Reinforce Vocabulary Skills at Home

## Tools and Reference

### Table of Contents

# Words in Another Country

**Note to Home** Use this page as a fun reference for pointing out the different words used for common objects in the United States and Great Britain. This will help your student begin to understand the cultural nature of words. You may wish to show your student where Great Britain is located on a map or globe.

Compare the American word to the British word for the same thing.

| American Words | British Words |
| --- | --- |
| cracker | biscuit |
| apartment | flat |
| principal | headmaster or headmistress |
| stove | cooker |
| soccer | football |
| sidewalk | pavement or footpath |
| raincoat | mackintosh |
| trunk (of a car) | boot |
| elevator | lift |
| windshield | windscreen |

Try putting the British word in place of the boldfaced American word in these sentences:

I like to eat **crackers** and jam.

Is there a **sidewalk** in front of your **apartment?**

The **principal**'s **raincoat** is bright green.

# Prefixes and Suffixes

**Note to Home** Read this page with your student. Use it as a reference for identifying words that have prefixes and suffixes in books you read together.

## Prefixes

A **prefix** can be at the beginning of a word.

| Prefix | Meaning | Example Word |
|---|---|---|
| pre- | before | preview = to view before (a movie preview) |
| re- | again | rewrite = to write again |
| un- | not; opposite | unlock = opposite of lock |
| | | unwanted = not wanted |

The teacher told me to *rewrite* my messy paper.

## Suffixes

A **suffix** can be at the end of a word.

| Suffix | Meaning | Example Word |
|---|---|---|
| -er | one who | farmer = one who farms |
| -less | without | tasteless = without taste |
| -ful | full of | joyful = full of joy |

The pretty music makes me feel *joyful.*

# Base Words

**Note to Home** Read this page with your student. Help him or her identify the prefixes or suffixes in the second list below (*-er, -ing, un-, -s, re-, -ed, -ness, -ly*). Extend learning by helping your student identify base words in books you read together.

A **base word** is a word without a prefix or suffix.

## Base Words

| | | |
|---|---|---|
| sing | wash | shy |
| lock | finish | equal |

## Words With Prefixes or Suffixes

| | | | |
|---|---|---|---|
| *singer* | *unlock* | *rewash* | *shyness* |
| *singing* | *locks* | *finished* | *equally* |

# Italian Words

**Note to Home** Many common words in the English language are borrowed, or adapted, from a foreign language. Use this page as a fun reference to help your student learn some American words that are also Italian words. You may wish to show your student where Italy is located on a map or globe.

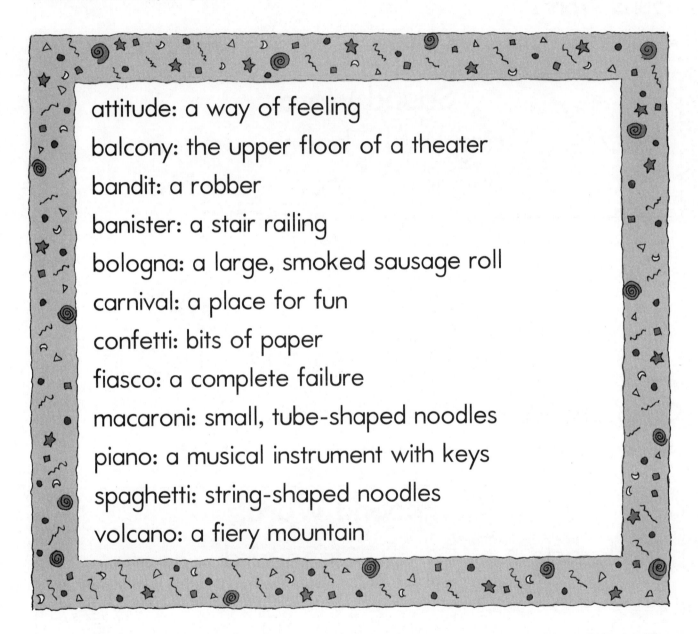

attitude: a way of feeling

balcony: the upper floor of a theater

bandit: a robber

banister: a stair railing

bologna: a large, smoked sausage roll

carnival: a place for fun

confetti: bits of paper

fiasco: a complete failure

macaroni: small, tube-shaped noodles

piano: a musical instrument with keys

spaghetti: string-shaped noodles

volcano: a fiery mountain

To keep from falling down the stairs, hold onto the **banister.**

We made **confetti** with colored tissue paper to throw during the parade.

# Fun With Words

**Note to Home** Read this page with your student. Ask him or her to identify objects or animals that match each sound word. Then help your student identify the two words in each compound word.

## Sound Words

A **sound word** is a word that sounds like what it means.

| Sound Words | | | |
|---|---|---|---|
| buzz | ring | boom | roar |
| chirp | quack | moo | hiss |

## Compound Words

A **compound word** is one word that is made of two words.

| Compound Words | |
|---|---|
| backpack | lifeguard |
| bookend | snowman |
| cupboard | seashell |
| skateboard | toothbrush |

# Dictionary Skills

**Note to Home** If you have a picture dictionary, refer to it as you read this page with your student. Help your student look up his or her favorite words.

A **dictionary** is a book that lists words and their meanings. Some dictionaries have pictures to show you what the words mean.

**canoe**

**nursery**

**tornado**

A dictionary may also show the word in a sentence.

*The children paddled their* **canoe** *down the stream.*

*My baby sister was asleep in her crib in the* **nursery.**

*The safest place to be during a* **tornado** *is in the basement.*

# Dictionary Skills

**Note to Home** Read this page with your student. Quiz him or her on alphabetical order by using the vocabulary words in this book. For example, "Which word comes first in the dictionary—*grip* or *ache?*"

## ABC Order

The words in a dictionary are in ABC order. This is also called alphabetical order.

A B C D E F G H I J K L M N
O P Q R S T U V W X Y Z
a b c d e f g h i j k l m n
o p q r s t u v w x y z

To find a word in a dictionary, you need to know its beginning letter.

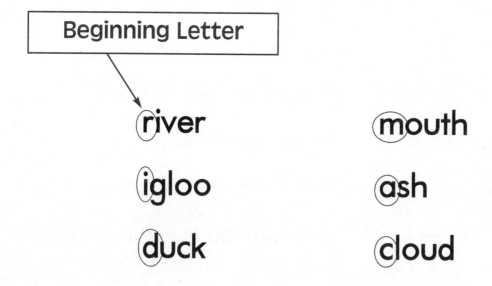

Beginning Letter

river        mouth

igloo        ash

duck         cloud

# Nouns, Verbs, and Adjectives

**Note to Home** Read this page with your student to introduce parts of speech. Choose a book that contains simple sentences, and lead your student in identifying nouns, verbs, and adjectives.

## Nouns

A **noun** names things, people, animals, or places.

| Nouns | | | |
|---|---|---|---|
| bowl | lake | thimble | garage |
| nest | penguin | soil | fish |

## Verbs

A **verb** shows an action or tells what something or someone is or has.

| Verbs | | | |
|---|---|---|---|
| roll | blink | pretend | fill |
| howl | obey | speak | drift |

## Adjectives

An **adjective** tells more about a noun.

| Adjectives | | | |
|---|---|---|---|
| silly | heavy | polite | rough |

*We made **silly** faces to make our teacher laugh.*

*The table is too **heavy** to move by myself.*

**Note to Home** The glossary provides a meaningful context for each vocabulary word presented in this book. Use it as a reference to reinforce your student's understanding of the vocabulary words.

# Glossary

## A a

**about** This book is **about** a green frog.

**above** We saw hundreds of stars in the sky **above** us.

**accident** It was an **accident** when I hurt my arm.

**ache** My fingers **ache** because I hurt them.

**adjust** **Adjust** your belt so it is not too tight.

**advance** I will **advance** one grade this year.

**airplane** People ride in an **airplane** high in the sky.

**alarm** We heard an **alarm** when we opened the fire exit door.

**alley** 1. We walked in the **alley** between the buildings. 2. We go to the bowling **alley** on Saturdays.

**almost** I **almost** dropped my cup, but I did not drop it.

**along** We walked **along** the country road.

**already** I was not hungry because I had **already** eaten.

**always** I **always** wash in the bathtub.

**among** They sit **among** other students at lunchtime.

**angry** The boy was **angry** when the toy broke.

**ape** An **ape** looks like a large monkey with no tail.

**arrive** My grandmother will **arrive** in Dallas at five o'clock today.

**ash** The wood in the fireplace burned to **ash**.

**ax** He used an **ax** to chop wood for our fire.

## B b

**backpack** I carry books in my **backpack**.

**baggage** Take only two suitcases as **baggage**.

**basket** We carried our lunch in a picnic **basket**.

**batch** We baked a **batch** of muffins.

**beautiful** The cat had **beautiful**, shiny fur.

**beaver** A **beaver** has sharp front teeth and lives by streams.

**bee** A **bee** is an insect that makes honey.

**begin** To **begin** means to start.

**behave** My dogs **behave** at home and do not bite.

**belong** You **belong** to your family.

**below** We saw snow on the road **below** our window.

**bent** He gently **bent** the tree branch, but did not break it.

**beyond** Our house is **beyond** those trees.

**bicycle** I put air into both tires on my **bicycle**.

**bird** A **bird** has feathers and lays eggs.

**blame** We **blame** our dog for the muddy floor.

**blanket** She lies under a **blanket** to keep warm.

**blessing** The rain was a **blessing** for the flowers.

**blink** To **blink** means to quickly open and close your eyes.

**blush** My face turns red when I **blush**.

**bookend** A **bookend** holds books in line.

**borrow** You may **borrow** the book from the library, but you must return it in two weeks.

**bowl** I eat oatmeal from a blue **bowl**.

**building** My mother works in a tall **building**.

**bunch** That is a big **bunch** of purple grapes.

**bundle** I tied the **bundle** of papers with string.

**bushel** A **bushel** is a way to measure grain.

**butterfly** A **butterfly** has a thin body and four wings.

# C c

**cabin** Abraham Lincoln lived in a log **cabin.**

**cage** My bird lives in a **cage.**

**canoe** We paddled our **canoe** down the river.

**canyon** A **canyon** is a deep valley with steep sides.

**carriage** The queen rode in a golden **carriage.**

**cart** A gray horse pulled the **cart.**

**cat** Our **cat** has whiskers and a long tail.

**caterpillar** A **caterpillar** looks like a short worm and turns into a butterfly.

**cave** The **cave** was a big hole in the rocks.

**ceiling** The **ceiling** of the room is above us.

**cellar** We store extra food and clothing down in our **cellar.**

**champion** Our winning team is the **champion.**

**chase** Our cat likes to **chase** mice in the field.

**chatter** The happy people **chatter** and talk.

**cheat** We do not **cheat** when playing games.

**child** The new baby is a young **child.**

**chimney** A **chimney** carries smoke away from a fireplace.

**chipmunk** A **chipmunk** has dark stripes on its back.

chirp  We heard the birds **chirp** outside.

circle  If I draw a ball, I draw a **circle.**

clerk  The **clerk** helped me find a new shirt.

cliff  We saw the valley from the top of a
    high **cliff.**

cloud  The **cloud** in the sky blocked the sun.

clown  A **clown** wears funny clothes and makes
    us laugh.

contest  My friend won the swimming **contest.**

coop  We keep our chickens in a **coop.**

cottage  We live in a **cottage** by the lake.

cousin  The child of your aunt or uncle is your
    **cousin.**

cover  A hat will **cover** your head.

cow  The **cow** was quiet when the farmer
    milked her.

crab  A **crab** has a hard shell and two claws.

croak  Big frogs sit and **croak** by the pond.

crowd  A large **crowd** of people waited to
    enter the circus tent.

cupboard  Our glasses and dishes are in this
    **cupboard.**

curve  A **curve** is a line that is not straight.

# D d

**daily**  **Daily** means every day.

**dart**  We saw a rabbit **dart** into the bushes.

**dash**  The dogs **dash** after the rabbit.

**dawn**  The sun rises at **dawn.**

**den**  The bear lay sleeping in his **den.**

**depend**  My birds **depend** on me to feed them.

**deserve**  You **deserve** praise for your good work.

**dew**  The **dew** on the grass made my feet wet.

**dining room**  We have dinner every night in the **dining room.**

**dish**  I put my sandwich on a **dish.**

**dodge**  Try to **dodge** the ball and not get hit.

**dog**  My **dog** barks and has floppy ears.

**double**  **Double** means two times as much.

**dove**  The **dove** made a cooing sound.

**dozen**  One **dozen** is a group of 12 things.

**drift**  We let our boat **drift** down the river.

**drowsy**  I feel **drowsy** when I lie in bed.

**duck**  A **duck** is a bird who likes water.

**due**  My book is **due** at the library today.

## E e

**east**  The sun rises in the **east.**

**effort**  Climbing a mountain takes a lot of **effort.**

**elephant**  The **elephant** picked up a peanut with its trunk.

**enough**  We had **enough** players for a baseball game.

**equal**  To be **equal** means to be the same.

**exact**  The clock shows the **exact** time.

## F f

**factory**  This **factory** makes farm machinery.

**fever**  He had a **fever** because his temperature was 102 degrees.

**field**  The **field** was full of tall corn.

**fill**  Please **fill** this glass with water.

**finally**  We **finally** got home after the storm.

**fine**  1. I had to pay a **fine** at the library.
2. The weather is **fine** today.

**finish**  Please **finish** your homework before dinner.

**fish**  The **fish** swam in the fishbowl.

**flat**  A piece of paper is very **flat.**

**float**  I can **float** on my back in the pool.

**fly**  1. A **fly** is a flying insect.  2. I like to **fly** my kite in the park.

**fog**  We could not see through the white **fog.**

**folks**  A lot of **folks** waited in line for a ticket.

**forest**  Many trees and plants live in the **forest.**

**frog**  The green **frog** hops into the pond.

**frost**  It is so cold that there is **frost** on our car.

**frown**  Her **frown** showed she was sad.

## G g

**gain**  You can **gain** strength by lifting weights.

**garage**  We keep our bikes and our car in the **garage.**

**gentle**  The **gentle** horse was easy to ride.

**giant**  1. The **giant** mountain was very tall.
2. The **giant** in the story was a tall person.

**giggle**  My sisters **giggle** at my jokes.

**glad**  I smile when I am **glad.**

**glory**  He gained **glory** when he won the race.

**grab**  Do not **grab** a bone from a dog.

**grandfather**  My **grandfather** is my mother's father.

**grandmother** Our **grandmother** is our father's mother.

**greedy** **Greedy** people are often selfish.

**greet** I **greet** you by saying "Hi."

**grin** I have a **grin** on my face when I am happy.

**grip** **Grip** the baseball bat with both hands.

**groan** I **groan** when I bang my foot.

**guess** You should **guess** the answer to a joke.

# H h

**handmade** My grandmother made me a **handmade** blanket.

**handsome** The **handsome** man had a nice smile.

**harm** It is mean to **harm** animals.

**heal** This bandage will help **heal** your cut.

**heap** A **heap** of hay lay by the barn.

**heavy** The chair is too **heavy** for you to lift.

**hide** I **hide** when I do not want someone to see me.

**hole** First we dig a **hole** for our seed, then we plant it.

**honest** I am **honest** and say what is true.

**hook** Please hang your coat on the coat **hook.**

**hoop** The lion at the circus jumped through the **hoop.**

**horse** The cowgirl rode her **horse** in the rodeo.

**hose** We water our garden with a **hose.**

**howl** Wolves and dogs both **howl.**

**hum** You can **hum** a song with no words.

**hurricane** A **hurricane** is a storm that begins in the ocean.

**hut** Their **hut** had a roof made of hay.

## I i

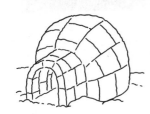

**ice** Water that is frozen is called **ice.**

**igloo** An **igloo** is a house made of ice and snow.

**ink** I write with the **ink** in my pen.

**inside** I put the food **inside** my mouth.

**instant** An **instant** is just a moment.

**island** An **island** is a piece of land with water all around it.

## K k

**knob** A **knob** is a round handle.

## L l

**lake** A **lake** is a body of water with land all around it.

**leak** The rain will **leak** through the hole in the roof.

**lifeguard** The **lifeguard** at the beach keeps swimmers safe.

**lion** The **lion** is a member of the cat family.

**live** Lots of animals **live** at the zoo.

**lucky** I was **lucky** to win a prize.

## M m

**mask** Wearing a **mask** makes your face look different.

**mean** You are **mean** to tease that dog.

**medicine** **Medicine** can help a sick person feel better.

**members** My cousins and I are **members** of the same family.

**mile** If you walk a **mile,** you walk 5,280 feet.

**minute** One **minute** has sixty seconds.

**monster** The **monster** in my dream scared me.

**motor** The fan's **motor** makes it blow air.

mountain  A **mountain** is much bigger than a hill.

mouth  I hum with my **mouth** closed.

music  We sing during **music** class.

## N n

nasty  Do not say **nasty** things about your little brother.

nature  The forests and the mountains are part of **nature**.

nest  There was a blue egg in the bird's **nest**.

nice  The **nice** girl was kind to everyone.

nightmare  A **nightmare** is just a bad dream.

north  Canada is **north** of the United States.

nothing  **Nothing** is scary to that brave girl.

nursery  A **nursery** is a baby's bedroom.

## O o

obey  When I **obey**, I do what I am told.

ocean  An **ocean** is made of salt water.

office  She works in an **office**.

on  Please put your books **on** the desk.

operator  The **operator** of a bulldozer should wear a hard hat.

outside **1.** I like to play in the park **outside.**
**2.** The **outside** of our house is blue.

overflow **1.** Water in a bathtub can **overflow.**
**2.** We can mop the **overflow** on the
floor.

## P p

page   I like the pictures on that **page** of
the book.

pain   I have a **pain** in my arm and it hurts.

pale   Your face looks **pale** and you seem sick.

paper   I drew a bird on my blue **paper.**

parent   A father or a mother is a **parent.**

pass **1.** You should **pass** the football to
another player. **2.** He threw a **pass** and
won the football game.

passenger   A **passenger** next to me on the bus
was sleeping.

past   Dinosaurs lived in the **past.**

penguin   A **penguin** is a bird that swims but
cannot fly.

pest   A **pest** is something that bothers you.

plow **1.** We watched the farmer **plow** his field.
**2.** The **plow** turned the dirt over.

plumber   The **plumber** fixed the leaking pipe.

**police**  The **police** help to keep us safe.

**polite**  Be **polite** and say "Please."

**porch**  There was a white swing on the front **porch.**

**pot**  She cooked the soup in a big **pot.**

**prairie**  A **prairie** is flat land covered with grass.

**prepare**  We must **prepare** for our trip by packing our bags.

**present**  **1.** The **present** is now.  **2.** I open my birthday **present.**

**pretend**  I like to **pretend** I can fly.

**print**  The names on the map are in small **print.**

**prize**  We won a **prize** at the school fair.

**promise**  When I **promise** to clean my room, I do it.

**puddle**  A small pool of water is a **puddle.**

## Q q

**quack**  The **quack** of a duck makes me giggle.

## R r

**rabbit**  A **rabbit** has long ears and soft fur.

**rag**  Use this old **rag** to wipe the floor.

**rain**  **Rain** falls from the clouds and waters the flowers.

**rainbow**  We saw the colors of a **rainbow** in the sky.

**ready**  We get **ready** to go to school in the morning.

**related**  My cousin and I are **related** to each other.

**repeat**  Would you please **repeat** your question?

**rest**  1. Remember to **rest** when you feel tired.
2. Did you get enough **rest** last night?

**return**  Please **return** this book to the library today.

**river**  We saw fish swimming in the **river.**

**roar**  The **roar** of the lion was loud.

**roll**  I trained the dog to **roll** over.

**roof**  The **roof** of the cabin was made of tin.

**rope**  1. I like to jump with this **rope.**
2. The cowboy **roped** the cow.

**rough**  A cat's tongue is **rough** like sandpaper.

## S s

**scooter**  A **scooter** has two wheels and a handle to hold on to.

**scratch** I had a **scratch** on my leg from the cat.

**seed** A nut is a **seed** from a tree.

**sentence** Write a **sentence** about your trip.

**shiver** The cold air made me **shiver.**

**shovel** 1. Use a **shovel** to dig a big hole.
2. We **shovel** the dirt into the hole.

**show** 1. The circus was a fun **show.**
2. You **show** your ticket at the gate.

**shy** My sister is **shy** and hides from visitors.

**silly** When I hear **silly** songs, I laugh.

**singer** My mother is a **singer** in the choir.

**sink** 1. We watched the sun **sink** below the hills.
2. Please put your glass in the **sink.**

**skateboard** A **skateboard** is a flat board with four wheels that you ride standing up.

**slap** Do not **slap** anyone in the face.

**smile** 1. A **smile** is a way to say "Hello."
2. Please **smile** for the camera.

**smoke** Only a cloud of **smoke** was left from the fire.

**snowfall** The **snowfall** today left heaps of snow.

**soil** The farmer planted seeds in the **soil.**

**sometime** She came here **sometime** last summer.

**south**  Mexico is **south** of the United States.

**speak**  To **speak** means to talk.

**spiral**  The **spiral** stairs curved around to the second floor.

**squeal**  I heard the pig **squeal** in the barnyard.

**stairs**  **Stairs** are steps that you can go up or down.

**story**  I wrote a **story** about tigers.

**straight**  The highway had a **straight** line down the middle.

**study**  My sister will **study** for her test.

**suddenly**  **Suddenly** we heard thunder.

**sunny**  The **sunny** sky had no clouds.

**support**  My mother will **support** me and take care of me.

**surprise**  A secret birthday party is a nice **surprise.**

# T t

**tale**  I like to read this **tale** of the wild west.

**tame**  A **tame** dog is not mean.

**tease**  It is not nice to **tease** people and make them cry.

**tent**  We sleep in our **tent** in the woods.

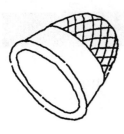

thank  I **thank** you for the present.

thimble  I wear a **thimble** on my thumb when I sew.

thin  The **thin** log was hard to walk on.

through  The mouse climbed **through** the tunnel.

throw  We **throw** the ball back and forth.

thunder  **Thunder** is the sound that follows lightning.

ticket  You need a **ticket** to ride the train.

tiger  A **tiger** is a member of the cat family.

tiny  An ant is a **tiny** insect.

tip  I sharpen the **tip** of my pencil.

toothbrush  I like to brush my teeth with a blue **toothbrush**.

tornado  A **tornado** is a storm with big winds.

tour  We went on a **tour** and saw the whole town.

tractor  The farmer rode a **tractor** in the field.

travel  I want to **travel** to Spain one day.

tumble  Penguins **tumble** and fall on the ice.

turtle  My pet **turtle** has a hard, green shell.

## U u

uniform  The police officer wears a **uniform**.

## V v

valley  A **valley** is low land between hills or mountains.

## W w

weed  1. We pulled the **weed** out of the flowerbed.  2. The farmer will **weed** his field.

west  Look to the **west** to see the most beautiful sunset.

wheelbarrow  Carry tools in this **wheelbarrow.**

whisper  I will **whisper** the secret to you.

wicked  **Wicked** people are not kind.

wide  No one could jump across the **wide** river.

wigwam  A **wigwam** is a house made of bark or animal skins.

wink  I close one eye to **wink.**

without  Do not read **without** your glasses.

## Y y

yawn  We watched the tired lions open their mouths and **yawn.**

# A—F Word Bank

# G—M Word Bank

# N—S Word Bank

# T-Z Word Bank